KT-521-586

ENDAL

Allen Parton is a Gulf War veteran who now devotes his time to charity and media work, along with his dogs, Endal and EJ. His wife, Sandra, works for Canine Partners, a charity that trains assistance dogs for the disabled. They have two children, Liam and Zoe, and live in Hampshire.

ALLEN & SANDRA PARTON

ENDAL

How one extraordinary dog brought
a family back from the brink

WITH GILL PAUL

harper
true

HarperTrue
HarperCollins*Publishers*
77–85 Fulham Palace Road,
Hammersmith, London W6 8JB

www.harpercollins.co.uk

First published by HarperCollins*Publishers* 2009
2

© Allen and Sandra Parton 2009

The Authors asserts the moral right to
be identified as the authors of this work

A CIP catalogue record for this book is
available from the British Library

ISBN 978–0–00–787349–4

Printed and bound in Great Britain by
Clays Ltd, St Ives plc

All rights reserved. No part of this publication may be
reproduced, stored in a retrieval system, or transmitted,
in any form or by any means, electronic, mechanical,
photocopying, recording or otherwise, without the prior
permission of the publishers.

Every effort has been made to trace the owners of copyright material
reproduced herein. The publishers would like to apologise for any
omissions and will be pleased to incorporate missing
acknowledgements in any future editions.

Mixed Sources
Product group from well-managed
forests and other controlled sources
www.fsc.org Cert no. SW-COC-001806
© 1996 Forest Stewardship Council

FSC is a non-profit international organisation established to promote the
responsible management of the world's forests. Products carrying the FSC
label are independently certified to assure consumers that they come
from forests that are managed to meet the social, economic and
ecological needs of present and future generations.

Find out more about HarperCollins and the environment at
www.harpercollins.co.uk/green

Dedication

To Liam and Zoe.

Also, to the 900,000 servicemen and women in Britain today who were injured serving Queen and country, and in memory of all those who didn't return.

Foreword

During the summer of 1999, a *News of the World* reporter in Havant, Hampshire, saw something he'd never seen before: a dog using a cashpoint machine. Right in front of him, a yellow Labrador inserted a card into the slot, waited while its owner, a sandy-haired man in a wheelchair, keyed in the PIN number, and then it carefully removed the card and the cash. The reporter blinked hard, wondering if he was hallucinating.

When he spoke to the man, a disabled ex-serviceman called Allen Parton, he found out that the dog's name was Endal and that using a cashpoint machine was just one of his many amazing skills. The *News of the World* article that followed seemed to fire the readers' imagination and soon many other newspapers, magazines, TV and radio shows were vying to find out about this exceptional dog.

They only learned a small part of the story, though. They thought they had found a performing dog, while in fact Endal was a one-off phenomenon, an unsung hero who had a profound talent for helping people in need. It would be a few more years before the full story emerged.

ENDAL

CHAPTER ONE

Allen

I opened my eyes. The room was fuzzy and the bright overhead lights were surrounded by blurred haloes. Something hard and uncomfortable was round my neck, digging into me.

'Are you all right, Allen? Glad to see you're with us again.' The voice was cheerful. A woman. I could make out her dark shape by the bed.

'Where am I?' I tried to say, but my throat felt tight and the words came out like a harsh coughing sound.

'You're in Haslar Royal Naval Hospital in Gosport. You had an accident, remember? In the Gulf?'

The Gulf of what? Gulf of Mexico? Gulf of Bothnia? Persian Gulf? Didn't this woman know how many gulfs there were in the world? And then I remembered. I'm in the Navy. I'm a Chief Petty Officer. I've been serving in the Gulf War.

'You flew back from Dubai overnight and got here this morning. You must be tired after the journey.'

I struggled to sit up and the nurse took my arm to help. I grabbed at the plastic collar round my neck.

'Better leave that for now until you've been checked over,' she said.

I wanted to ask when I would be seeing a doctor, but my mind went blank on the word 'doctor'. What were these people called again? The ones with stethoscopes, who told you what was wrong with you?

'Medical …?' I stuttered, then a compulsive twitch made my shoulders shudder.

She answered for me: 'A doctor will be round to see you shortly. Do you want to have a wash first?'

I nodded yes, and swung my legs round to put my feet on the floor. Everything about the way I was moving was odd and unconnected. My body felt as though it belonged to someone else and I was struggling to control it. What was going on? I leant on the bedside cabinet to push myself up and noticed there was no sensation in my hand or arm, only a kind of pins and needles.

'The toilet is this way,' the nurse pointed. 'I think I'd better come with you.'

'No!' I waved her away rudely and forced my left foot to take a step forwards, then followed with the right. I had to think consciously about each step, willing my feet to move. This was very strange.

In the bathroom, I pushed the door shut and leant against it, breathing heavily with the effort of crossing the room. There was a mirror opposite so I lurched across to peer into it.

I looked more or less the same: a bit tired maybe, but otherwise OK. There was a large bruise on my temple that felt tender when I pressed it. The neck collar was grubby, as though I'd been wearing it for some time.

I splashed water on my face, trying to remember what had happened and why I was there. I'd been in an accident in the Gulf, she said. What kind of accident? Nothing at all came back to me. I must have had a bump on the head. That would explain the bruise. Well, it would all come back later, I decided.

When I emerged, a doctor came over to watch me walking across the ward. 'That looks like a bit of a struggle,' he said. 'How are you feeling?'

'Strange,' I slurred.

'Can you remember your name?'

Of course I could. Whom did he think he was talking to? 'Chief Petty Officer Parton,' I barked out, the words sounding all mangled and muddled.

'And the name of your ship?'

I opened my mouth to reply and realized I had no idea. It had gone. I shook my head blankly.

'Do you know what age you are?'

I racked my brains. My mind raced back over countries I'd seen, ships I'd sailed on, weapons systems I'd helped to design, but I couldn't think what age I was.

'Missiles,' I said, trying to communicate to him that that was my job.

He nodded, and then guided me to the bed where he began to examine me, taking my blood pressure, shining a torch in my eyes, pricking my arm for blood. It hurt. Why couldn't he have done it on the right side where I seemed to have no feeling?

'What's happened?' I asked eventually.

'We think your brain has had a traumatic injury. There's no damage to the skull. It's all internal.' He made some notes on his chart, then folded his arms. 'I don't think there would be any point operating. We have to wait till the inflammation dies down and we'll see what happens next.'

I was irritated. Just do your job, I thought. And get me back to work. I haven't got time to sit around here for weeks on end. My men need me.

'The staff nurse will give you something for the pain. Take it easy now.' He turned and walked off.

I blinked. Yes, there was pain. My head and neck were aching. I let the nurse help me back on to the bed and swing my feet up for me.

'Lunch will be round in a bit,' she said. 'Then your wife's coming to see you later.'

I stared at her blankly. I had a wife? That was news to me.

She frowned. 'You don't remember, do you? Her name's Sandra. You'll know her when you see her. She's been very worried about you.'

She left me to digest that news. I lay back on the pillows trying to trigger my memory. Wife. Wedding. Married. I was married. I could remember that it was a good thing to be

4

married. You were in love, and you looked out for each other. But I had no memories of my wife at all.

And then visiting hour came, and a very attractive woman with dark hair and a curvy figure was hurrying across the room. I peered hard as she came into focus. She was definitely heading towards me. It must be her.

'Allen,' she said. 'Oh my God.' She kissed me and looked into my eyes. 'How are you feeling?'

And I thought she seemed like a nice person, but she was a complete stranger to me. I didn't remember ever seeing her before, never mind marrying her. I had no feelings for her whatsoever. Inside my head there was a vast fuzzy blankness.

CHAPTER TWO

Sandra

Allen sailed off to the Gulf in April 1991, leaving me at home to look after our two children: Liam, aged six, and Zoe, aged five. It was always hard when he went away but after seven years of marriage I was beginning to get used to it. It goes with the territory when you're a naval wife. However, this was the first time since I'd met him that he'd been posted to a war zone, and although the fighting was over and Saddam Hussein's troops had been chased out of Kuwait, I was still nervous. Every time I read news stories about random shootings, friendly fire incidents or that missile that hit a military base in Saudi Arabia, a knot tightened in my stomach.

I'd been suffering from anxiety and panic attacks since I had a severe case of post-natal depression following Zoe's birth. Some days I found it hard to look after myself, never mind two children, and I struggled to cope with all the incessant chores and responsibilities that come with running a house. Allen was my rock during that period, the person who could always calm me down and make everything all right. He'd walk in the front door and cook us all a nice meal, and whatever I was stressed about, he'd say, 'Don't worry. I'll take care of it. I'll go and get the shopping, I'll pay the bills, I'll pick the children up from school.' He was a calm, capable, very caring kind of man.

Now that Liam was at school and Zoe's difficult baby years were past, I was managing a lot better but I still missed Allen very badly. Silly things, such as the central heating breaking down or one of the kids falling and scraping their knees, could reduce me to a panicky wreck again. He called from the ship when he could, but it was a complicated process. He had to book a call in advance, wait to get a line, and then if I happened to be out he would miss his slot. I had no idea when he would be back in the UK. We were hoping that he would be home for Christmas but there were no guarantees. There never were.

Then tragedy struck when my sister Valerie died of liver failure on Monday 12 August 1991. For most of her adult life she'd been battling complex health issues, but the end came suddenly and shockingly and I was distraught. Right up to the last moment we hoped she would pull through but it wasn't to be. She left behind a little boy who was just five, two months older than Zoe, and it was a horrible family tragedy.

I contacted the Navy's Family Services and asked if I could speak to Allen urgently. They called the ship and a few hours later he was able to ring me briefly.

'I'm so sorry,' he said, his voice breaking up across the crackle of international airwaves. 'I just wish I could be standing there right now with my arms round you.'

I started crying so much I could hardly speak. 'Please come home, Allen,' I begged. 'Please.'

'I'll put in a request with Family Services. We should know soon. When's the funeral?'

'I don't know yet. Early next week.'

'I'll do my best to get there. I love you,' he said. Then the line was abruptly cut off.

'Love you too,' I sobbed into the vast distance between us.

I'd never needed him more in my life, but the next day I got a call from Family Services to say that he couldn't get leave because it wasn't a member of his family who had died.

'It's his sister-in-law!' I cried. 'He was very close to her.'

'I'm afraid that's not considered a close relative in Navy terms. If it was his own sister that would be different.'

I argued but they had made up their minds, so I just got on with trying to deal with it myself, along with my mum and my two remaining sisters Marion and Jennifer. There were the funeral arrangements to make, Valerie's little boy to look after, her possessions to deal with; it was all too much on top of caring for my two lively kids. I staggered through each day, barely coping, just doing the minimum because my energy levels were so low. It was as though there was a huge weight pressing down on me making it virtually impossible to do anything.

Every day I prayed that Allen would at least be able to get access to a phone to ring and see how I was. Even a few words of comfort from him would have helped. I'd never felt so utterly alone. My sisters and my mum were immersed in their own grief and couldn't deal with mine as well, and the kids were just too young to understand.

The following week, on 21 August, I got another phone call from Family Services. When I heard who it was, I assumed they were calling to see how I was managing after Valerie's death and couldn't make sense of what they were saying at first.

'We're calling to tell you that Allen's back in hospital again,' a woman's voice said.

'What do you mean he's *back* in hospital?' I was stunned.

'After his accident,' she said.

My heart started pounding hard. 'What accident?'

I heard an intake of breath. 'Didn't anyone call you? Last week. He was involved in an accident. He's OK, but he's had a bang on the head.'

'*When* last week? Why wasn't I told?'

There was a rustle of paper. 'Last Friday, the sixteenth. I thought you knew. I'm sorry. He was admitted to hospital with concussion but then the ship was sailing and they didn't want to leave him behind so they took him back on board to treat him there. But I suppose his condition has deteriorated a bit so he's been transferred to a hospital again.'

'Where is he? I need to speak to him. Do you have a number I can call?' I needed to hear him tell me what had happened in his own words.

'I'll have to get back to you on that. But honestly, don't worry. It doesn't sound serious.' She was embarrassed and obviously couldn't wait to get off the phone.

Honestly, don't worry? Straight away I got on the line to HMS *Nelson*, the naval base he was attached to, but no one there seemed to know anything. They all just promised they'd get back to me. I paced the house waiting for the phone to ring. Zoe was playing with a jigsaw on the floor and when Liam got in from school they started fighting with each other. Kids always seem to sense when you are anxious, which makes them seek even more attention, which just adds to your stress. I suppose I could have phoned and asked a friend to come round and keep me company but I didn't want the line to be engaged when Family Services called me back, nor did I feel like talking to anyone. I just had to keep myself busy until I found out what was going on.

I was making the kids' tea when I finally got a phone call, but it wasn't exactly the information I'd been waiting for.

'You'll have to call the British Embassy tomorrow morning and they'll arrange for a call to be put through to your husband's hospital ward.' They gave me the number.

'How is he?' I asked. 'Is there any more news?'

'No more news. Just that he's had a bump on the head. Try to keep yourself busy and don't worry about it too much.'

I thought, Yeah, right, you do that when it's your husband. I just needed to speak to him and hear in his voice that he was OK. I'd trained as a nurse and knew that head injuries could cause a wide range of symptoms from a simple raised lump through to inflammation of the brain and all sorts of complications. I couldn't understand why he hadn't tried to call me himself since the accident. Yes, it was difficult to get access to a phone, but surely the circumstances were exceptional?

When I finally got through to the hospital in Dubai, a nurse with a heavy accent said she would get Allen on the line. I waited and waited, trying not to think about how much a phone call to the Middle East must cost per minute. It sounded as though nothing was happening and I was about to hang up when I suddenly heard breathing down the line from thousands of miles away.

'Allen, is that you?'

There was a pause. 'Yes, it's me. Who are you?'

'It's me! Sandra.' I guessed it must be a bad line at his end. 'How are you? What's happened?'

'Well, I haven't got any clothes,' he said.

'What do you mean?' Was this a joke?

'I haven't got anything to wear.' His voice sounded panicky.

I frowned. 'You must be wearing something just now. Won't that do?' In the Navy they often lived in the same set of clothing for weeks on end and just learned to live with the smell of themselves and each other. Besides, Allen wasn't the kind of person to bother about having a clean set of clothes. If he only had one pair of underpants for a week, he'd joked to me, he'd wear them right way round, wrong way round, back to front, upside down, and make do.

'I've got no clothes,' he repeated.

I was starting to get alarmed. 'Allen, what's happened? Why are you in hospital?'

'I don't know why I'm here. I can't remember.'

I asked more questions but couldn't get anything out of him. He just kept returning to his anxiety about his clothes.

'I have to go, darling,' I said at last. 'This call is costing a small fortune. I'll ring you back tomorrow, OK?'

'Right, bye!' he said and the line went dead.

This was very strange behaviour, and not like him at all. Our international phone calls were precious and we always ended them by saying 'Love you!' but he hadn't given me time. He hadn't asked about Valerie's funeral or how I was coping or mentioned the kids. This was all so stupid. It felt unreal, as if it couldn't be happening. I started phoning around everyone I could think of to find out what had happened, but I just kept hitting blank walls. No one seemed to know.

I hardly slept a wink; my stomach was tight with anxiety and my thoughts raced through endless possibilities. The next day I called the hospital again, hoping to get more sense out of Allen, but someone I presumed was a nurse explained to me that he'd been moved.

'Where to?' I asked.

'We don't know,' came the reply. 'You'll have to ask his ship.'

I rang the British Embassy, and after some delay they called back to tell me that he was in a hotel room in Dubai. It was two hours before I could get through to him, and we had another brief, bizarre phone call in which he sounded vague yet on edge.

'Someone's stolen my stuff,' he said.

'I'm sure they haven't. It'll be on the ship waiting for you.'

'It's gone,' he said, slurring a bit, which I presumed must be a side-effect of the painkillers he was taking.

He still didn't seem to have a clue how he had been injured. It was most peculiar.

'Should I fly out to see him?' I asked the woman at Family Services. 'I could find someone to look after the children for a few days.'

'There's no point in you going out because I think they are planning to medevac him home.'

'When will that be?'

'We don't know yet.'

I had a conversation with an officer at the base, who said something I found very strange. 'We've got no idea what he was doing off the ship that night. He and a friend seem to have gone ashore without permission and been involved in a car accident.'

'But how is that possible?' I asked. 'How did they get off the ship? Where would they have got a car from?'

'We don't know. We're running an investigation and we'll find out more in due course.'

I didn't believe for one second that he had gone AWOL. First of all, it would have been totally out of character for my ambitious, responsible husband, and secondly, I knew how difficult it was to get on and off naval bases. Whenever I went to pick Allen up after work at *Collingwood* or Rosyth or wherever he was, I had to get through strict security, showing photo passes and being noted and documented. You didn't just wander on and off ships at will, especially in a war zone. There had to be more to it than that.

During the next two weeks, I only had a few more worrying phone calls with Allen, but dozens of frustrating calls with the naval authorities, without getting to the bottom of what was going on. I seemed to get different people every time, so I had to explain the situation from scratch, then they'd go off saying, 'We'll have to see if we can find anyone in the office who knows anything about this.' It was all horribly frustrating. My husband was injured overseas and I couldn't be with him and there was nothing I could do to help.

I tried to keep myself busy, doing endless housework, cooking, sewing, covering Liam's school notebooks with coloured paper – anything to keep my mind occupied. I couldn't bear silence and stillness because then the anxiety fluttered in like a big black moth. If they were going to med-evac him home that meant the injury must be serious. Head injuries can cause brain damage. Why had he sounded so odd when I spoke to him?

'He'll be fine,' I told people who asked. 'We just need to get him back in this country for some proper TLC.' If I said it often enough, I could try to believe it.

On 7 September I was told that he was at last being flown home to the UK. I was desperate to see him, and pleased that I would be able to do so soon, but deeply apprehensive about what condition he'd be in.

A random thought occurred to me: this might be a ruse on Allen's part to get the home leave we'd requested and been denied after Valerie died. Could he have put his career on the line by faking injury in order to get back and support me? Allen was a bit of a comedian, with a taste for practical jokes. He'd say, 'Do you think this smells funny?' and you'd lean in and next thing whatever it was would be on your nose, and I used to fall for it every time. But I knew he was far too much of a professional to fake an injury. That couldn't be it.

I so wanted for him to walk in the door and make my life better. I needed looking after since Valerie had died. I needed my husband.

Once again I was pacing the house, waiting for news. At last the call came to say that his plane had taken off and on arrival in the UK he would be admitted to Haslar, the military hospital in Gosport, where I could go in to see him the following day.

I tossed and turned, wide awake all night long, and my heart was in my mouth as I drove the few miles to the hospital. I couldn't wait. I was as nervous as a teenage girl on a first date.

I found the ward and picked him out straight away, sitting up on top of his bed and wearing a neck brace. He saw me at the same time and watched as I walked across the room, but he didn't smile at me or wave hello.

'How are you?' I asked, and kissed him on the lips. There was a big bump on his temple that looked more recent than three weeks old. 'How did you get that bump?'

'Fell,' he said, and the word was oddly slurred.

'When did you fall?'

He thought about this and shrugged.

'How are you feeling?'

'Funny,' he said, and I could hear it was an effort to get the word out. He was almost barking, forcing his throat to emit sound. Then he twitched compulsively, his right shoulder jerking and his face contorting.

I looked into his eyes but could see no spark of my husband, my rock, the man who always looked after me. He looked blank. There was something seriously wrong.

'You've been on an overnight flight,' I said soothingly. 'You're probably just tired.'

He twitched again, a kind of irrepressible shudder. I chatted a while longer then went to find a doctor. 'What's wrong with my husband?' I demanded. 'I'm a nurse and I'd appreciate it if you'd tell me straight.'

'We don't know exactly,' he said. 'There's obviously been some trauma to the brain and we're keeping him under observation and running tests.'

'How did he get that bruise on his temple?'

'I'm told he fell the day before yesterday. Have you seen him walking yet?'

I shook my head.

'He's having significant problems controlling his legs. We'll just have to keep an eye on it all. Meanwhile, I see no reason why you can't take him home for the weekend. With your nursing background, you should be able to care for him.'

'Are you sure?' I asked, feeling hopeful. Surely he couldn't be too bad if they were letting him out?

'Why not? Just bring him back on Monday morning and he can see a consultant then. Have a nice family weekend together.'

The doctor smiled and I felt reassured. Everything was going to be all right. They wouldn't let him home otherwise, would they?

A nurse and I helped Allen to get dressed and walk down to the car. On the way back to the house, I drove slowly and cautiously. I did all the talking, telling him about Valerie's funeral and the children and everything that had been happening, but I got no response at all. He closed his eyes and I couldn't even tell if he was listening, so after a while I stopped and drove in silence.

As we pulled into our street, I said, 'The kids are really excited about seeing you. They're at Julie's but I said I'd go and get them as soon as we arrived.' Julie was my wonderful next-door neighbour who had four kids of her own but was always happy to look after my two as well. 'Two more don't make any difference at all,' she'd laugh.

Allen turned to look at me and I couldn't read the expression in his eyes but he didn't seem enthusiastic about seeing the kids. Maybe he wasn't feeling well enough.

'Why don't we go in and get settled first?' I suggested, and he nodded. He'd hardly spoken throughout the journey, and when he did his speech was very slow and indistinct and he was often lost for the most basic words.

We pulled into the driveway and I walked into the house behind him, noticing that he had an odd, rolling gait. He picked his right foot up high and flopped it down then pulled the other one through. It reminded me of the way the actor John Thaw walked. He'd had polio as a child and would pick his foot up and put it down with a strange precision. As a nurse, I'd always noticed that about him.

Allen plonked himself down on the sofa and sat looking around him.

'Do you want something to drink?' I asked.

'Yeah.'

'Do you want tea or coffee?'

He screwed up his face, unable to think. 'The stuff that comes in bags,' he slurred.

Tea, then.

At that moment there was a burst of squealing and running feet and the children erupted into the house.

'Daddy!' they shrieked, over the moon to see him. Zoe leaped on to his knee and Liam snuggled on to the sofa beside him.

'Get off me!' he snapped loudly as he pushed Zoe away. The look of bewilderment on her little face was heartbreaking.

'Kids, Daddy's not feeling very well. Don't climb all over him.'

'I've got a new train, Daddy,' Liam said excitedly. They used to play together with his Playmobil train set.

'And I've started ballet,' Zoe joined in, not wanting to be left out. 'And I've got a new dolly as well.'

'Go away!' Allen snarled, putting his hands over his ears.

They were devastated. Whenever Allen had come back from postings in the past, he'd burst in the door bringing them presents, swinging them in the air and tickling them. They just didn't have a clue what had happened.

'Daddy's got a bad headache,' I said gently. 'You know what it's like when your head hurts. Just leave him in peace for a little while and maybe he'll play later.'

I sent them over to Julie's for the afternoon, just telling her briefly that Allen wasn't very well. When I got back, he was examining two tubes of cream he'd been given on prescription. He had a nasty rash on his feet and another one on his groin and they'd given him a different cream for each rash, but he couldn't remember which was which. There was nothing written on the boxes and he was very anxious about it.

'Which cream is which?' he mumbled. 'I don't know.'

The old Allen would have made a joke out of it. He'd have said, 'I'll start by putting them on my feet because if my feet fall off that will be fine, but I don't want the other bits to fall off.'

But he was incapable of joking now.

'I'll go to the pharmacy and ask them,' I offered. 'Let me just get your tea first.'

Two minutes later, as if I hadn't spoken, Allen asked, 'What about this cream for my feet? What am I going to do?'

It was like being with an old person who had Alzheimer's. When I worked in a nursing home, some of the residents would ask the same question over and over again – usually: 'When is my daughter coming? Why's she not here yet?' That weekend Allen asked me about his creams at least twenty times a day and he never seemed to hear the answers I gave.

I showed him the photos I'd had developed from a holiday we'd had in Singapore and Penang just a couple of months earlier, but there was no spark of recognition. He didn't seem to remember us being there and I thought that was very worrying. He just looked at each one and handed it back to me without comment.

He didn't seem to remember where anything was in the house either. I had to show him where his clothes were kept, where his shaving stuff was and how to turn on the shower. My sense of alarm grew stronger by the minute.

It was a sunny weekend so I set up a chair for him in the back garden and he just sat there twitching and rubbing at his rash and fretting about his creams, and a knot tightened in my stomach. This wasn't my Allen. It was as if a stranger had taken over Allen's body. How long would this last? When could I have my intelligent, loving husband back?

I couldn't wait to get him to Haslar on the Monday morning so that they could start treating him. Despite all my nursing training, I felt utterly helpless. I had no idea what I could do to help him. Whatever it took, I would do it – but I didn't have a clue where to even start.

CHAPTER THREE

Allen

Over the days and weeks after the accident, I realized that I had lost a huge chunk of my memory. Doctors reassured me that it was a common side effect of head injuries and was often just temporary but I sat obsessively trying to work out what I could and couldn't remember. In particular my entire childhood was a blank, so I asked Sandra to tell me what she knew about it.

She said that when I was a kid I lived in a council house in Haslemere, Surrey, with my mum and my sister Suzanne. Mum and Dad split up when I was two years old and we lost contact with Dad, which must have been really tough for Mum. She struggled to cope financially and we didn't have lots of toys or fancy bikes, parties or trips to the zoo, but there was always food on the table and clothes on our backs. In my teens, I got a boarding-school place paid for by the council and that helped to ease the burden.

My gran lived in London where she used to work for Sir Samuel Hood, the Sixth Viscount Hood, who came from a family long associated with the Navy. At Christmas time, Lord Hood used to let us come up to London and stay with my gran in his house in Eaton Square while he and the family were out at their estate in the country, and seemingly I was in awe of the place. There were huge oil paintings on the walls, of battleships at Trafalgar and great storms at sea, and all kinds of naval memorabilia like sextants and charts and telescopes. Sandra says I told her I used to love just standing in front of them staring and pretending I was on deck, clinging to the rails as huge waves lashed the sides. Much of his collection is now housed in the Royal Naval Museum in Greenwich, I believe. Anyway, I'm sure it was there that I formed my ambition to join the Navy. It must have been an exciting environment for a young boy.

Sir Samuel heard about my plans and offered to send me to Officers' College, bless him, but I decided I would rather work my way up from the bottom. I suppose I thought the officers' school would be full of toffs and I wouldn't fit in. It's not that I wasn't ambitious, but I wanted to have hands-on experience at every level. I never wanted to be one of those people who know how to calculate the volume of a biscuit tin but have no idea how to open it.

So I signed up when I was just sixteen years old, did my basic training, where you learn how to march, clean your uniform and all that sort of thing, then I went to HMS *Collingwood* naval school at Fareham in Hampshire, where I was given technical training in electrics, radar systems and basic mechanics. I joined my first ship, HMS *Hermione*, at Portland in Dorset and we were thrown straight into war exercises, which is real 'Boy's Own' stuff: they were launching thunder flashes at us, turning on the mains and flooding compartments, setting things on fire – all the things you would never normally be allowed to do on board – and we were forced to deal with it. We had to use our mattresses to plug holes in the side of the ship, and rescue 'wounded' civilians, and it was all a huge adventure. If this was meant to be work, I was all for it.

After that I set off on a year's cruise round the world, following the kind of itinerary you'd pay tens of thousands of pounds for as a tourist. The most vivid early memories I have now are from this tour of duty; there are clear pictures in my mind of many of the places we visited. We went down past Gibraltar, through the Panama Canal, up to San Diego and Vancouver, then across to the Far East, Singapore, and right round the globe. Whenever we docked somewhere, I'd catch a train and go exploring instead of sitting in the nearest pub getting hammered, as some of my shipmates were prone to doing. I went to Disneyland and Las Vegas and all the major tourist attractions, and I met some wonderful people along the way.

I remember sitting in a pub in Gibraltar one sunny afternoon, with the monkeys playing on the Rock above us, and I can tell you exactly what I was drinking and what we talked about. I remember going through the Panama Canal with nothing but dense jungle towering on either side of the ship. I remember flying in a seaplane from Vancouver Island to the mainland and seeing the plane that had gone just before us ditching head-first into the water. And I remember Singapore back in the days when it was rough and ready round the docks, with beggars hustling you and taxi drivers jostling for your custom and all the old buildings that have been knocked down now to make way for pristine glass skyscrapers.

Mum wrote to the captain of my ship to complain that she never heard from me and he called me in for a chat. 'Send her a postcard from every port,' he told me. 'She's your mother, after all.' I didn't want to waste time writing great screeds so I got into the habit of sending a card that just had one word on it: 'Hi!' She has a huge collection from all over the world, and all of them just say 'Hi!', but that seemed to keep her happy. I got the odd letter from her with news from home, but I didn't get homesick or miss her, as I know some of the other young lads did. I was having the adventure of a lifetime and I'd left Haslemere way behind me.

It was a bit of a shock when we got back from our trip to be told that we were being sent out to Northern Ireland, which in the late 1970s was a dangerous place to be. The Navy didn't have to do battle on the streets, but the Army guys we met were all very jumpy. I was based at a transmission station near Belfast called Moscow Camp, where I had to do maintenance schedules for all the weapons systems and check that valves were working and so forth. I never saw any direct violence but I was aware that a lot of the guys I bumped into were virtually in shock about what was happening, living in an environment where bombs were just coming over the walls and there could be a terrorist round any corner. I suppose it was the same as is happening in Afghanistan today. You see guys drinking meths on the streets of London, and when you question them you hear that they were soldiers who came out of Northern Ireland so traumatized that they were never able to readjust to normal civilian life.

I was a bit of a swot, always putting myself up for exams, and before I left HMS *Hermione* I'd achieved my first promotion. I'd go and sit on the beach with all my reference books and huge carrier bags of notes, and I'd study and study. In Gibraltar I found an old gun emplacement – a pillbox, we call them – and I'd sit there and boff up. Promotion meant rank and more pay, so I always put myself up for any advancement I could, although you had to be a particular age before you could sit some of the exams. Lots of friends I'd joined up with couldn't be bothered – they were happy just to do the job and weren't looking to be an officer one day – but it was always an ambition of mine.

Gradually, I was put in charge of other men, and I think I was pretty fair as a boss. I was always willing to give everyone who came up the gangplank a chance, even if I knew he had been kicked off another ship. I'd say, 'There's your weapons system, there're the maintenance schedules, I want you to paint it, clean it, oil it, grease it. If you need help, ask me. It's your job now, but if it doesn't work it's down to you.' And, by putting my trust in someone like that, I often found I'd get the best-maintained system on the ship. When a guy who's made a mistake is given a second chance, he's not going to mess up again.

I made my men work really hard, and the only punishment I used for misdemeanours was making them stick little round hole-strengtheners on all my files. We had huge books of drawings of the wiring of all our different systems, known as BRs ('books of reference'). This was in the days before microfiches and computers were widely in use, of course. I didn't want the paper to tear where holes were punched, so if the guys did something wrong I'd sit them down with a huge pile of sticky hole-strengtheners and make them do both sides of each page. I heard the lads called them 'paper arseholes', which made me smile.

I was really committed to the job – if there was still work to be done, you'd never find me slipping off to a pub onshore – and I reckon I dealt with it and my men pretty well. I saw the young guys who had gone straight into the officer-training course, usually from comfortable backgrounds where Mummy and Daddy took care of everything, and I knew I'd made the right decision to work my way up the ranks. They didn't have an iota of experience, and yet they were supposed to be in charge of men who had huge family problems, divorces, sick children, money worries, and they had no idea what to do. It was better to be a big fish in a small pond than a small fish who was thrown right in at the deep end of the big pond, in my opinion.

I had a fantastic time along the way, on all the different ships I was posted to. The life could be very glamorous. I remember I spent six months in the Great Lakes between America and Canada on the biggest ship that had ever made its way in there. As we approached through the locks, the huge wicker fenders on the ship's sides caught fire due to the friction, the fit was so tight. We were there as a kind of exhibition ship. Models like Jerry Hall came to do shows on the helicopter flight deck, wearing spindly high heels that tended to get caught in the mesh of the deck covering.

We sailed to Chicago, Milwaukee, Duluth, and everywhere we went there were flash parties with champagne and cocktails. We flew the ship's helicopter over Niagara Falls, and I remember we stopped in Montreal on the way back up the St Lawrence River. I have a vivid memory of climbing a huge set of wooden steps there, up from a park to a place where there were stunning views right up and down the river for miles and miles. I've searched for it in Google Earth and I can find the park but I can't find those steps, and that drives me crazy because then I start doubting myself and wondering if I'm just imagining them. But I'm sure I'm not.

That was all before I met Sandra. I have no recollection of how we met, where we met, what I said to her that night, or what I thought about her at the time. I don't remember what we did on our first date, the first time we kissed, jokes we shared, how we fell in love or when I asked her to marry me – none of that stuff remains. I know what she's told me but I have no first-hand memories at all, which is very distressing for her and just plain weird for me. She's shown me albums of photos from our wedding and it's strange to see myself there, happy and smiling and obviously very much in love, but to have no recollection of it at all.

I know that soon after we were married, in 1983, I was posted up to Rosyth in Scotland. We had married quarters that looked out over the Forth Road Bridge and the view was amazing. My job was to maintain the minesweepers and repair any other ships that came in with problems. The regular crew would go on leave and we'd go on board with the books and check all the maintenance and fix up the bits that weren't working and then hand it back to the crew once they were rested. We were there for a year, I think, and then we were transferred down to Portsmouth where I worked on a guided-missile destroyer.

The kids were born in these years, first Liam in 1985 and then Zoe in '86. Apparently, the night Zoe was conceived I was meant to have been at sea, but the ship's engines broke down so we came back ashore, and she was the result!

After Portsmouth, I was moved to Bath, where I was working for the Director of Engineering Support, basically designing new weaponry systems. There was a vast underground naval complex beneath the city, which was like something out of a Harry Potter novel, and we didn't see daylight from Monday to Friday. It was dark in the morning when I started and dark when I walked out in the evening, but I loved the challenges of the work I was doing.

I was the only non-commissioned officer there. I'd passed the exams and so forth but I hadn't actually gone to Dartmouth to get my commission, and I was aware that I was being watched by all the other officers to see whether I fitted in. When we went out socially, the highest of the high were watching my social graces, so I couldn't make myself a chip butty at table or anything like that. I had to wear a jacket and tie instead of running around with the lads. But I was ready for it. Being an officer would mean that I could provide better for my family.

When the Gulf War started in 1990, after Saddam Hussein invaded Kuwait, I volunteered straight away. I felt I should be out there on a ship instead of sitting behind a desk in Bath. It was never going to be a naval battle, so it was more about making sure supplies were getting through to our troops, intercepting any shipments of arms to the Iraqis, that kind of thing. We didn't need thousands of ships there because it was all fairly easy with modern radar equipment, and you can more or less see right across the Gulf anyway.

When we arrived, our ship was given some free fuel from a prince who owned some oilfields in one of the Gulf States and we found we weren't really needed, so we sailed on to Singapore and Malaysia. I know Sandra came out and joined me there, because she has shown me some stunning pictures of us standing in front of huge Buddhas and going round all the sights. So in fact, when she waved me off to go back to the theatre of war, we were sailing from Malaysia, not the UK. That was the last time she saw the 'old me'. I've got a complete blank about that whole period. I can't remember a single thing. I've no memory of ever being in Malaysia or the Gulf. It's all gone. Sometimes I think I remember things because I've seen a picture of them but I can't fill in any detail that's not in the picture.

When I woke up in Haslar military hospital in September 1991, I was determined to get straight back to work. I just needed the doctors to fix me up. I hadn't had an operation, there weren't any scars or blood and gore, I hadn't broken my back or my neck, so why was I having such trouble walking?

'Your brain is not sending signals to your legs,' I was told. 'That's why they don't respond effectively. There's nothing actually wrong with them.'

It was the same with my eyes. There was nothing the matter with them, but because my brain wasn't working properly it wasn't picking up signals from the optic nerve as efficiently as it should have been. The squint I'd had as a young child appeared to have come back. And I had no feeling in my right arm and the right side of my body, although I seemed to be able to move them; there were intermittent pins and needles but I couldn't feel my hand if I dug a nail into it.

I took hope from the fact that there was no physical damage. Surely I just needed a bit of rest and it would all come back again? But why did I seem to have forgotten roughly 50 per cent of my life history? I had no memories of my grandfather, mother, sister, wife or children. Why did I forget basic words like 'toothpaste' and 'bed' and 'pyjamas'?

'You experienced a huge traumatic internal brain injury when your spine was forced up into the brain cavity,' they said. 'There's no treatment we can give you. We just have to wait and see. It could get better, or it could get worse.'

If the doctors ever sounded negative in their prognosis, I thought to myself: They don't know whom they're dealing with. Maybe other war veterans would sigh and shrug and accept their disabilities, but I was way too ambitious for that. I was itching to get back to my career. I would work tirelessly at my physiotherapy and speech therapy and any other damn therapy they cared to give me. I would keep exercising until my legs worked properly again; I'd recover my memory and my speech and my eyesight and I'd astonish them all with my miraculous powers of regeneration.

I was so determined that I didn't listen to anyone who warned me it might not be possible to get back the life I'd had before. They didn't know me. They didn't have a clue what I was capable of. As far as I was concerned, they were just plain wrong.

CHAPTER FOUR

Sandra

Allen and I met in November 1982 in a nightclub in Haslemere, Surrey. I was twenty-three years old and living near there in a village called Clanfield, where I was working as a live-in nanny for the children of a surgeon at the hospital where I'd trained as a nurse.

I liked nursing on the whole and knew I wanted to end up working in some kind of caring profession, but I'd recently been posted on a couple of difficult wards, including a unit for people with severe burns, which had been very traumatic and upsetting. I decided to take a bit of time out from nursing to decide what to do with my future, and the nanny job was ideal. I got on really well with the surgeon's wife, and when I mentioned to her that I was finding it hard to meet new people in the area she arranged for me to go to the nightclub and be introduced to some of the locals by the club owner, who was a friend of hers.

'I need to get you up to that naval base and meeting some of those young officers,' she said, prophetically.

I tried on lots of different outfits and spent ages doing my hair and make-up that night. It seemed like a long time since I'd made the effort, and the surgeon's wife sat and chatted to me as I got ready. I was very apprehensive about turning up at a club on my own, even though she said the doorman would look after me when I arrived. I'd led quite a sheltered upbringing and wasn't really a clubbing type. The whole thought of it made me feel very awkward.

My shyness wasn't helped by the fact that when I arrived the doorman who was supposed to be looking after me wasn't there, but I hadn't been in the club long before a scruffy-looking guy in ripped jeans and a tatty old duffel coat came up to me, completely the worse for wear.

'You've got beautiful eyes,' he said. 'Will you marry me? I'm pregnant, and I need you to marry me or I'll get into trouble with my mum.'

I thought it was a great opening line, and liked his handsome boyish looks and the twinkle in his eye.

He told me his name was Allen, and then he bought me a hugely potent cocktail called a JD, which had orange juice, angostura bitters, gin and vodka in it, together with something else completely lethal, I think.

I was definitely attracted to him but I didn't much like the fact that he was drunk. I've never been comfortable around heavy drinkers, having grown up with an alcoholic father.

As his speech grew more incoherent and I saw he was having trouble standing upright, I made my excuses and walked away. I didn't want to have to mop up after him if he was sick! But in the week that followed I found myself thinking about him and wondering if I'd see him again. Despite the alcohol, he definitely had charm.

The following week I went back to the same Haslemere club, hoping to see him, and was delighted when he came bounding over as soon as I walked in.

'I'm sorry if I said anything rude last week. I hope I wasn't too offensive.'

'I'm surprised you even remember meeting me,' I commented.

'How could I forget that I was talking to the most beautiful girl in the room?' he said, and I blushed. 'Do you want to come and join me and my friends?'

'All right,' I said shyly.

We got chatting and I decided I liked him when he was sober. He was playful and engaging and there was definitely chemistry between us. I was very pleased when he asked if I'd accompany him to a cheese-and-wine evening at the naval base the following weekend.

As the week went by, however, I got a bit nervous. What should I wear? How formal was it? Allen had said he would book a bed and breakfast for me near the base in Fareham, but would he expect to stay over with me? I wasn't sure yet how I felt about that. I knew I liked him but I didn't want to rush things.

As it turned out, the evening was fantastic. Allen had booked a taxi to pick me up from my B & B. He met me at the gate, took my arm as we walked in and behaved like a perfect gentleman all night. It was the first time I'd seen him in uniform and he looked very attractive, not to mention sexy. I liked the fact that he held doors open for me and took my coat and went to the bar to get me a drink, and that he introduced me to all his friends. Everything went smoothly and being with him felt very natural.

Afterwards he came back with me to the B & B, and even though I hadn't known him for long I asked him in to stay the night. It just felt right. The surgeon's wife had given me half a bottle of champagne and we shared it over whispered conversation before we went to bed. Next morning, he had to sneak out early before the landlady saw him because he wasn't registered as a guest. The sight of him tiptoeing down the stairs in his socks, shoes held aloft, trying not to make a noise, was hilarious.

We started seeing as much of each other as we could: we went to the pictures, had dinner together, walked in the countryside, and talked the whole time. I couldn't stop thinking about him between dates and used to get a churning in my stomach when he called, or when I was on my way out to meet him. He was the most interesting, lively man I'd ever met, and I could tell he was a nice guy underneath the extrovert exterior. He definitely had a caring side.

Allen explained that he could get a posting at any time that would mean he'd have to go overseas, and I told him plainly that I wasn't going to wait around being 'the girl he saw when his ship happened to be in Fareham'. I was at a stage in my life when I knew I wanted a husband and a home of my own and I didn't want to waste time on a relationship that wasn't going anywhere. I also knew I was falling in love with Allen and I wanted to be sure I wasn't going to get my heart broken.

Fortunately he seemed to feel the same way because it wasn't long before we started talking about marriage. Allen wanted to do it all properly though. At Easter 1983, just four months after we met, he was booked to go skiing in Switzerland with five of his friends. He'd learned to ski in the Navy and was seemingly very good. He suggested that I came along and shared the chalet with them, then he could propose to me formally out there, against the dramatic backdrop of snow-covered mountains. Before we left, he went to see my dad and asked his permission, which was a typically old-fashioned, gentlemanly touch.

I'd never skied before but I picked it up quite quickly and really enjoyed myself. Allen was a brilliant skier, whizzing down the slopes like a streak of lightning. It was a shame it wasn't just the two of us but he had already arranged the holiday with his mates from the Navy and couldn't cancel.

We'd talked about it and I knew he was going to propose at some point but he wouldn't tell me which day he was going to do it. The way it happened was incredibly romantic. We'd just got off the chairlift at the top of the mountain and were carrying our skis to the top of a run, with a stunning view spread out below us, when Allen got down on bended knee in the snow.

'I love you, Sandra, and want to spend the rest of my life with you,' he said. 'Please will you do me the honour of agreeing to be my wife?' He produced a very pretty diamond ring from the pocket of his ski suit.

I was on the verge of tears. 'Yes, I will,' I said straight away. I loved his perfect manners and the way he could always make me feel so special. It couldn't have been a more beautiful proposal.

That night, though, we went out to a local restaurant with his friends and they decided to celebrate by getting smashed. As the evening wore on, they grew more and more raucous until the owner of the place finally asked them to leave. Allen's friends couldn't understand why I didn't like heavy drinking, and obviously thought I was a killjoy. They even tried to spike my drink. I was humiliated and angry, and really I thought we should have been having dinner on our own that evening.

The next morning, I was still tetchy with Allen and, sensing it, he became tetchy back. It all blew up when I asked him to brush the snow off my ski boots and he refused, snapping, 'Do it yourself.'

That was it. My temper finally erupted. I pulled the engagement ring off my finger and hurled it into the snow.

'In that case, you can forget all about getting married,' I snarled.

We had a furious stand-up argument, in which I yelled at him that he had ruined our engagement by getting drunk. 'I grew up with a father who always smelled of booze. He was scary and unpredictable when he was drunk and there's no way I'm going to marry a man who drinks too much.'

'I don't drink too much. I just know how to let my hair down and you don't.'

'No, and I don't want to if it means getting thrown out of a restaurant. I don't want to live like that.'

I knew in my heart of hearts that Allen wasn't an alcoholic. He just liked having fun with his friends. He was gregarious and obviously very popular with the other lads, whereas I was quieter and more reserved, but somehow we complemented each other.

'That wasn't my fault,' he said, and blamed one of the other lads. 'He's just back from the Falklands where he saw friends of his killed and maimed, and he needs to let off steam.'

The whole time we were arguing, I kept my eye on the spot where the ring had landed, right in the middle of a snowdrift. I'd wanted to make a point but I didn't want to lose it.

'Come on,' he said finally. 'Can we kiss and make up? I'm sorry we ruined your evening and I promise I'll make it up to you.'

I felt safe with him, and life was always fun when he was around, so there was no question that I would forgive him. We both got down on our hands and knees and scrabbled around in the snow until I found the ring, sparkling away in the sunlight. Allen slipped it back on to my finger and we fell into each other's arms.

We'd planned to wait a year before getting married, but in August 1983 he was told he was being posted overseas. If we got married first, I could go with him and we'd be allocated married quarters, so that's what we decided to do. It was only after we were already committed that they told us the posting was going to be Scotland rather than some far-flung sunny place as I'd hoped. Meanwhile, I had just three months to plan and organize a wedding for around a hundred people, so it was all a bit frenzied and chaotic.

We wanted to get married in a big Italian church in Wilton, the town where I grew up, and the only date it was available when Allen was also free was 5 November. It was a very traditional wedding, with my sisters, nieces and nephews in the bridal party. My sister Jenny made all the bridesmaids' dresses and it was so cold in the church that she left room for everyone to wear thermal vests underneath. I saw a beautiful picture in a wedding magazine of some swans made out of choux pastry and asked the local bakery to recreate them but on the day they came out looking like Loch Ness monsters rather than swans. Everyone said how appropriate that was since we were going to Scotland.

The day flashed past for me. We had the reception at the Pembroke Arms hotel opposite the church, and then we dashed off to catch an overnight sleeper up to Scotland just as everyone around the country was enjoying their bonfires and fireworks displays. Allen's friends entered into the spirit of the night by putting bangers in the exhaust pipe of our car and placing kippers in the car heater, which wafted out intense fishy smells during the journey.

Our honeymoon consisted of a week together in Scotland in naval quarters, where we had no heating, no TV and single duvets on the bed, but it gave us the chance to explore a bit. After that Allen had to go off on a training course and I went back down to my mum's, so it was 16 December 1983 before we moved into our first marital home together, a lovely three-bed maisonette in Rosyth with views over the Firth of Forth. I found a job working at a local hospital and joined the fitness club for naval wives, and started to get used to my new life.

We decided to get a dog as we both loved them. Allen had had pet dogs as a boy, and our shifts could be juggled so that it would never be left on its own for more than a couple of hours. We went to the Rescue Centre together and picked out a scruffy black Labrador cross, who was about four or five months old. We reckoned he was probably an unwanted Christmas present. No matter how much you tried to tidy him up, he always looked messy and disreputable, so the obvious name for him was Scruffy. He was a spirited and demanding dog from the start, but we enjoyed taking him for long walks in the surrounding countryside, and shared the responsibility for his care with each other.

Around June 1984, they wanted to give me a routine chest X-ray at work and asked if there was any chance I could be pregnant. I had come off the pill and my periods were a bit erratic so I didn't think there was, but they decided to run a pregnancy test to be on the safe side and, to my complete astonishment, it was positive.

I couldn't get through to Allen on the phone to tell him, so I went to Mothercare and bought a tiny babygro and when he walked in the door that evening I just handed it to him and said, 'Guess what?'

He was over the moon – we both were. We thought the Rosyth posting was going to last three years and Allen would be on shore so it was an ideal time for us to have a family. But only a week later we were told that the following April he would have to leave his job there and go to sea on a ship that was based in Portsmouth. I was beginning to experience one of the realities of life as a naval wife: unpredictability! Whatever plans you make for the future, you always have to be ready to change them at the drop of a hat.

Almost exactly a year to the day after moving to Scotland, by now heavily pregnant, I turned around and had to move back down to Portsmouth in the week before Christmas. There was all the palaver of packing up our stuff, finding acceptable accommodation, transporting the dog and changing my antenatal appointments from one hospital to another.

Baby Liam was born on Valentine's Day 1985 and thankfully Allen was able to be with me. Nurses make terrible patients. As I lay in pain in the maternity unit, I noticed that the nurse looking after me had put the straps in the wrong place and I kept worrying about when they were going to give me the promised epidural. Would they be too late? Then the nurse confessed that she hadn't delivered a baby for twenty years and was on a refresher course, which didn't do a lot for my confidence! But all went well and I brought home my beautiful little boy.

Allen was fantastic in those early weeks. I fed the baby and he did everything else: nappy changing, winding, housework, meals for us, laundry, shopping. He was always good around the house, and he obviously doted on Liam as well. He had a real knack with babies.

Sadly, Scruffy the dog wasn't quite so good. After the move he began chewing things and being generally obstreperous. If I was going out, I had to leave him shut in the kitchen, but the final straw came when I got home one day to find he had chewed up the entire base of the door frame in our rented house. I realized I just couldn't cope any more. Allen was due to go to sea when Liam was ten or eleven weeks old and I knew I couldn't manage a destructive dog and a new baby at the same time. We agonized over it but I was feeling very tired and run down after the birth and I didn't have the energy to try and retrain a boisterous dog. If Allen had been there we would have managed together, but it just felt like too much for me on my own, so finally we agreed that Scruffy would go back to the RSPCA. When we phoned them, they were in no doubt that they would find another home for him quickly, and that settled it.

Allen was quite upset about it, especially since he was away on the ship when the call came to tell me to take Scruffy in to their kennels so he never got the chance to say goodbye. I was sad too, but my overwhelming emotion was relief that I wouldn't be clearing up the mess any more and could focus on my new baby.

Liam was only a few months old when I discovered I was pregnant again. It was totally unplanned and a huge shock, if I'm honest. I was still learning how to cope with one baby and couldn't imagine doing so with two. How did other women ever manage?

I put my back out really badly during the pregnancy, while carrying Liam on one hip and wheeling a shopping trolley across a supermarket car park. My entire spine just seized up and I couldn't even get Liam into his car seat. I had to place him on the floor of the hatchback boot and drive home really carefully, and then get a neighbour to carry him into the house. A midwife came round and told me I needed complete bed rest, which is easier said than done when you've got a one-year-old crawling around the house. Allen took some time off to help, but that meant he didn't get so much leave when Zoe was born, which was very hard on both of us. My sister Marion came to stay for the first couple of weeks, and returned whenever she could take days off work, but I still had to manage most of the time on my own.

Liam had been a lovely lazy baby, who slept through the night at five days old, took his feeds well and was happy to have a nap whenever you put him in his cot. Zoe was more difficult, though. She flatly refused to feed from me after about two weeks. I started to bottle-feed her, but if I took the teat away to wind her she wouldn't have the same teat back again. Feeding her was a complex business, and she cried a lot.

She'd had a very quick delivery and, looking back, I think she may have suffered some trauma during the birth, so perhaps she was in pain. Nowadays I might have taken her to a cranial osteopath but I didn't think of that back then. All I knew was that she wailed endlessly and nothing seemed to calm her. At night I'd walk round the house holding and rocking her, then in the daytime I'd put her in the car and take her out for a drive to try and get her to stop crying and go to sleep.

Meanwhile I had Liam crawling round my ankles, having to be watched constantly in case he tried to stick his fingers in an electric socket or bashed his head. Allen was away on a long trip right through this period and I had no idea when he would be back. I was sleep-deprived, my back still hurt, the housework started to pile up and I felt increasingly desperate. I've always been someone who copes, who just gets on with things, but I knew I was reaching my limits.

Then one morning, Zoe just cried non-stop. She refused to feed, she didn't want cuddles, her nappy was dry and I was at my wits' end. I put both babies in the car and drove round for an hour but still she wouldn't stop crying. I lifted her out of the car in her car seat to bring her back into the house, and suddenly it all got too much.

'Will you just shut up?' I screamed, and I shook the car seat as hard as I could. Immediately afterwards, I put the seat down and sank on to the floor beside it, horrified at myself. What if I had hurt her? She was still crying but not so loudly. It was then I knew I needed help. This couldn't go on.

I called the health visitor and she came round to visit. At first she tried to be reassuring, saying that it was normal for a new mother to find it difficult to cope, especially with two so close together. She said she thought it sounded as though I had post-natal depression and maybe I should get some anti-depressants from my doctor. It was an interesting thought that hadn't occurred to me. I'd assumed it was all my fault, that I was doing something wrong or I just wasn't suited to motherhood, but maybe there was a physical cause. Maybe I wasn't going mad after all.

'I'm scared that I might really hurt her,' I said, and told the health visitor about how I had shaken Zoe's car seat.

She listened quietly and asked me more questions about exactly what happened. I think she must have been seriously worried because she went off to make some phone calls then came back and said: 'It might be a good idea to give you a break for a couple of weeks so you can catch up on your sleep and get your strength back. How would you feel if we took Zoe into temporary foster care?'

I was shocked to the core. Did that mean she didn't think I was capable of looking after my baby? Having a child taken into care seemed a terrible stigma.

'Just think of it as a bit of help with babysitting. You'll be able to visit her whenever you like, but these people are experienced parents who should be able to get a feeding and sleeping routine established for you. She can come back home as soon as you're feeling better.'

I was flooded with anxieties. What would Allen say? Would he think I had failed as a mother? Is that how everyone would see me? But I couldn't think of an alternative, so I agreed.

My doctor diagnosed me as having severe post-natal depression, and said he thought it had started after Liam's birth and got worse after Zoe's. I was relieved to have a cast-iron excuse for my behaviour, but still desperately ashamed that I had been unable to cope.

The foster family were very kind people. They lived nearby so I could go round and visit Zoe whenever I wanted. She stayed there for five or six weeks, and after she came back to live with me again they continued to look after her one day a week to give me a break. I genuinely don't know how I could have got through that period without their help.

Still, it was several months before I could scrape myself back up off the floor and manage to feed both babies, get them in the car and go down to the local shops for some groceries. It was hard even to get out of my dressing gown some mornings. I worried that people would be watching me the whole time for signs that I was cracking up, and that they would be keeping an eye on the kids to look for bruises or signs of malnutrition. I'd lost confidence in my ability to care for myself, never mind these two alien little beings. I felt anxious whenever I had to go out of the house and started having panic attacks over the least little things, but gradually, with lots of help from my doctor and health visitor and those wonderful foster parents, I got back on track again.

Allen came back to work on shore when Zoe was a year old, but he was based in Bath from Monday to Friday and we only saw him at weekends. With that job he was promoted to Chief Petty Officer, and in 1987 we moved to a nicer house in a place called Emsworth, between Chichester and Portsmouth. Once the kids were at nursery school I went to work part-time in a nursing home on Hayling Island, and I really enjoyed it there. You can make a big difference to someone's final years by finding the time to stop and chat with them, doing their hair and such like, and it was a fulfilling job for me. It helped to make me feel like a capable person again, so was very good for my battered confidence.

When Allen announced in 1990 that he'd volunteered for the Gulf War, we didn't discuss the possibility of him being killed or injured but I suppose it was in the back of our minds. I resigned from my job and during the last weeks before he left we spent a lot of quality time together with the kids. They'd just got bikes so we taught them how to ride them. We had day trips to London and a holiday in Center Parcs and we had loads of fun, but always with the shadow of the war hanging over us. I'd switch off the TV or radio if the news came on to avoid hearing about any casualties or helicopter crashes or the speculation that was rife at the time that Saddam Hussein might use poison gas against our troops.

Some of my favourite family memories come from that period when it was just the four of us enjoying time together.

Allen hadn't come from a particularly close family, but I always thought it was important to get down on the floor and play with the kids, to take them on outings, and for us all to have special family Christmases and celebrations together. I liked creating a close-knit unit, with our own family jokes and traditions and games. I've got lots of pictures in my head of us all smiling and messing about in those last weeks before he set sail, and they're very precious.

Allen set off in April, but in early July I was invited to go and join him for a holiday in Singapore and Penang. I was reluctant at first because I'd never left the children for any length of time before, but my sister Marion offered to have them and finally I said I would go. I wrapped a little gift for them to open each day that I was away and I phoned them as well, but it was hard for me to leave a five-year-old and a six-year-old. They were still so young. In retrospect, however, I'm so glad I did have that last, very special time in the sun with Allen, just the two of us. The memories are bitter-sweet but I'm so happy I have them to treasure.

We'd talked about the future before, but I remember we had more discussions about our plans while we were in Malaysia. Basically we decided that I would continue to move around following Allen's postings until the children were at secondary school, at which point I would stay in one place with them so their education didn't suffer. A lot of naval kids went to boarding school but I wasn't in favour of that; I wanted to keep them at home with me till they were at least eighteen. Allen would serve his contractual twenty-two years with the Navy; then we would decide where we wanted to live and buy our dream home there. We'd only be in our forties and we could start a whole new life doing whatever we wanted.

It's ironic, I suppose. I think it was John Lennon who said, 'Life is what happens when you're busy making other plans.' I knew Allen was going into a war zone but the Navy weren't supposed to be directly involved in the fighting because it had been a ground and air war, driving the Iraqi army out of Kuwait, and now the main action was over and they were just on peacekeeping duty. It never occurred to me that Allen might be injured because of that. Anyway, he was too good at his job. I suppose I couldn't even contemplate him being hurt because I needed him so much. He was the stable one, and I was still prone to bouts of anxiety and depression that he helped to pull me out of. That was the dynamic of our relationship at the time.

And then the news of his accident filtered through and everything changed overnight.

CHAPTER FIVE

Allen

It was a huge shock the first time Sandra took me home for the weekend after the accident. I'd overheard them saying that she was a nurse but I was still anxious she wouldn't know how to look after me properly. Shouldn't there be a doctor there as well? What if I needed help with things like undressing myself? Would this woman do it? Was she really my wife?

Then, in the car, she mentioned that we had children, and that was most peculiar. I didn't feel like a person who had children. I had no memory of them, no idea of their names or what ages they were.

When we got back to the house, I didn't remember any of it, but there were photos of Sandra, the children and me all over the walls so I knew I was in the right place. When would my memory come back?

Then the door opened and two children burst in shouting and squealing. I couldn't bear the noise they made. I didn't feel as though I was their father. There was no bond there, no memories of when they were babies; they were strangers, and the two of them seemed to make the noise of twenty children. It drilled into my ears and echoed round my head.

'Go away!' I waved my hand, and Sandra came rushing out, concerned. 'Go away!' I gesticulated at her as well. My speech was thick and slurred but I could tell they understood me.

I had a horrible itchy rash that was spreading up my body and itching constantly and I fretted about that most of the weekend. Could it be a strange tropical disease? Had I contracted something in one of the hospitals they'd put me in? Was it an allergic reaction to the medication I was on? Or was it a symptom of some serious new development in my condition?

I hated being helped to get dressed, all my food being served for me, and the fact that there was very little I could do. I'd flown all over the world fixing battleships at the drop of a hat, and now I couldn't make a cup of coffee for myself because my hands kept twitching and it would have spilled everywhere.

I found that I couldn't remember words. I could bark out an order – such as 'Coffee!' – but when I noticed a cake on the countertop and wanted a piece, I couldn't remember the word for it to ask for some. Sometimes I'd try and I'd confuse Sandra by coming out with the wrong word – 'kite' or 'door' perhaps. Or I'd just point and growl. I certainly couldn't speak in sentences, or remember any of the niceties such as 'please' and 'thank you'.

Sandra was incredibly patient that weekend. She tried to jog my memory by showing me photos from a holiday we'd had in Singapore and Malaysia. I recognized myself in the pictures and I could tell that we looked happy in them, but they brought back no emotions. I didn't remember being in that place. I only felt frustration at the barriers in my brain, huge impenetrable walls that I couldn't bypass.

A doctor had explained to me that after it's been damaged the brain favours some types of memories over others. The 'favoured areas' are different for everyone. Some might keep their love of music, or sporting prowess, or the ability to do complex mathematical calculations. As for me, I think I retained a lot of my technical knowledge, because I could remember precise details about the weapons systems I'd worked on in my various postings for the Navy, but I'd lost all my memories of the people in my life.

The problem is that memories are the basis for emotions, and love is based on shared history, and because I couldn't remember any of our history I no longer felt any 'love' for Sandra and the kids. I'd woken up and found myself living in the middle of a life that didn't feel like mine. It didn't feel right. It was as though I was visiting strangers and I didn't feel well enough to be polite or friendly to them.

I couldn't actually remember what 'love' felt like. How did you know when you loved someone? I knew nothing about the woman and the two children who were trying to get through to me. They were strangers. It's maybe a bit like watching a man in his eighties who has dementia and is being cruel to his partner because he can't remember who she is. I had a sort of reverse dementia and I just felt emotionally blank, like an empty shell.

Sandra's nursing experience may have meant that the staff at Haslar let her take me home, but after observing me close up for a couple of days she realized that I wasn't fit to be there. I needed specialist help that she couldn't give me. She took me back to Haslar on the Monday morning and had a chat with the staff and before long I was being transferred to Headley Court rehabilitation centre near Epsom in Surrey for assessment. And that's where I stayed on and off for the next year, just coming back to visit Sandra and the children at weekends.

Originally an Elizabethan farmhouse, Headley Court was converted into a huge mansion by Lord Cunliffe, governor of the Bank of England, in the early twentieth century. During the Second World War, Canadian forces were based there, and the grounds were used for army training exercises, then after the war money was raised to convert it into a rehab centre. They have doctors, nurses, physiotherapists, occupational therapists, speech and language therapists, a cognitive therapist, and several hydrotherapy pools and gymnasiums, as well as workshops where they make artificial limbs.

'Right!' I thought when they showed me around. 'Let's get started.'

* * *

An orderly handed me a newspaper. 'Here you go, Allen,' he said brightly. 'Just have a read through and pick out a story that interests you. Any little nugget will do. When I ask you later, you have to try and remember what it was you picked out. OK?'

I grunted and opened the newspaper: the *Sun*. Every morning in Headley Court they brought you a paper and asked you to memorize a single item. The *Sun* had little square boxes of two-line stories: simple things, like amazing animal feats, or vicars who streak through their churchyards. I picked one of these and repeated and repeated it in my head, over and over again.

The other patients were sitting round the day room scanning their own papers but I tried not to look at them, focusing hard on remembering my news item. I ignored the other voices and the general chatter about the day's news, and I tried not to look at anyone else.

Then the orderly turned to me and asked, 'What was your story today, Allen?'

I opened my mouth – and it was gone. Just a blank space where the words had been minutes before. I shrugged, furious with myself, and turned to glare out of the window.

'Not to worry. Maybe tomorrow,' he said. 'Now, who can go round the room and tell me everyone's names? Do you want to have a go, Dave?'

Dave would love to. He always got it right. He pointed at each person and said their name, and when it came to me he said, 'Dolly Parton,' which was my nickname in the Navy.

And I hated Dave at that moment. I was full of rage that he could do something I couldn't. We both had severe head injuries and were struggling with a range of disabilities, but his short-term memory for facts seemed better than mine and his speech was certainly a lot better, and I didn't think that was fair.

Dave was an RAF instructor and had been injured in France. He'd been cycling all the way from Catterick, North Yorkshire, to Gibraltar, when he was knocked over in a hit and run. At Headley Court, Dave could always remember his news item in the morning and he could remember everyone's names and the latest football scores, but on Sunday evenings he'd ask: 'Has my mum been to visit me this weekend?' even though it was only an hour or so since she'd left. He couldn't remember that. They got him a little notebook that he kept by his bed, and he was supposed to write down everything that happened in it so he could keep track.

'Look at your book,' someone would say whenever he asked about his mum.

Dave was in a bad way so I should have been more charitable but I really hated him when he did better than me at those memory games. It wound me up that we had to do them every morning and I always failed.

I often thought that if you had to have a brain injury, it would be better to have a more catastrophic one so that you no longer retained any awareness of your state. The worst thing was that I knew I wasn't stupid. I could remember that I'd had a very high-powered job designing weapons systems for the Navy. I had flashes of complete memories, but they were like tiny islands in a vast dark sea. I couldn't put them in order or get them to join up, but I knew that I used to have a lot of people working under me, and that thousands of colleagues relied on my expertise every time they went to sea. I'd worked my way up through the ranks, serving in Northern Ireland, in the Falklands, and then in the Gulf War. I'd passed my boards to become an officer so I'd had a glittering career ahead of me with good pay and prospects. But now I couldn't remember one paltry item in a newspaper for half an hour. It drove me nuts.

After the newspapers and the 'naming game', the orderlies handed out boxes of Lego along with pictures of things we were to try and build. I'd loved Lego when I was a boy. I think it had just been brought out then, and I got one of the first-ever sets. I also liked Airfix models and model railways – anything technical, basically. In Headley Court, they gave us a two-dimensional picture of the three-dimensional object we were supposed to make with the Lego, along with some instructions, and it was supposed to stimulate your cognitive powers. I could never follow the instructions, though. I had to do it my own way, figuring it out for myself, often working backwards, and usually I'd get there in the end, even if my model wasn't 100 per cent perfect.

As I struggled with Lego blocks, memories would come back to me of sophisticated weapons systems I'd used and helped to develop. For example, in the Falklands War in 1982 we'd been testing an anti-submarine torpedo system. A huge missile was fired from a ship and when it reached the point where it detected a submarine, the torpedo was dropped with a parachute attached, and it searched the area until it found its target. We fired a practice one at an American submarine from a range of 150 miles, and it was so accurate it dropped directly into the conning tower and they couldn't get their hatch open. It had special telemetry so that we could see what had happened during the flight, whether any equipment had been damaged during take-off and so forth – it was quite an impressive piece of machinery.

I peered at the picture of a Lego ship I'd been given, trying to work out how to make a mast, and the irony made me feel very bitter. From someone who was in charge of high-tech weaponry, I was now back in my second childhood, dependent on carers and struggling with the most basic tasks.

'Bollocks!' I muttered as part of the prow broke off and fell to the floor beyond my reach. I swore a lot, and that was the word that seemed to come out most often.

Most days we had some kind of workshop. If it wasn't Lego it might be twisting a bit of wire to make a metal coat hanger. They handed out the wire, the instructions and the finished product, but I found I could never follow the written instructions. I got the lefts and rights and back and front muddled and it just hung loosely apart, no use to anyone. However, when I examined the finished product and worked backwards I could see exactly how to do it. I took my wire and copied the existing one and eventually got through the task.

Another day we had to put together a bird table. I can't imagine they let us use saws and power drills, not with all the neurological disorders in that room. They probably gave us the pre-cut pieces and we had to assemble them in the correct order.

I saw a speech therapist most days because my words were coming out like a bark or a harsh cough, and I had the most terrible stutter that was painful to listen to. We had to go back to basics and retrain my voice box, tongue and lips with a laborious series of exercises so that I could get words out clearly – if I could remember them, that was. I still forgot lots of words, and I still resorted to snapping 'Bollocks!' in my frustration, but the speech therapy started to help, and that was a positive step.

The physiotherapists worked out a programme for me to try and deal with the spasms that caused me to twitch and flinch so frequently. I'd lost a lot of weight during the weeks of bed rest and my muscle tone was poor but I threw myself into a compulsive exercise routine. I found that I could swim using my upper body strength, and I could lift weights and raise myself up on the climbing wall. I began to exercise during every free moment of the day until the doctors had to come and speak to me about it.

'Allen, you're losing too much weight with all this exercising. You need to calm down. If you get any thinner, we'll have to send you to hospital and get you on an intravenous drip.'

I rejected what they said, though. I thought, Fit body, fit mind, and still sneaked off to the pool or the gym whenever I could. I saw some of the other guys getting fat with enforced rest in a wheelchair or bed, and I was determined that was never going to happen to me. I'd never been overweight in my life and wasn't about to start now.

There had been some books in the bag of possessions Sandra brought along for me and I tried to read one of them, but it was no good. By the time I got to the end of a page, I'd have forgotten the beginning and would have to go back and remind myself who the characters were and what it was all about, so I gave up before long. I practised and practised reading newspapers, determined that one morning I would pass the memory test, but to no avail. No matter how many ways I tried to fix a story in my head, it just wouldn't stay there.

I tried writing, but it came out all wrong, with the characters back to front, for example, and that was very alarming. You need to be fastidious when you work on naval weapons systems and you couldn't afford to put a '3' the wrong way round or switch a '6' for a '9'. But I just couldn't see the characters in my mind's eye any more, because you need memory for that. It got to the point where I wanted to punch the therapists – it was the speech therapists who worked with me on my handwriting – even though I knew they were only trying to help.

It seemed that I was hitting brick walls with everything I tried. When was I going to start getting better? Why couldn't they give me some drugs, or even do an operation to get me back to normal again? This was all taking far too long.

Occasionally we'd be taken for days out. We were bussed off to Birdworld once, a huge park where they had lots of aviaries, and you could watch penguins being fed and see herons doing tricks. I wanted to walk round on my own but the orderlies insisted that we all stayed together and didn't wander off, as if we were a bunch of schoolchildren. That was really irritating.

The other thing that annoyed me was in the coffee shop when a stupid waitress turned to one of the orderlies and asked, 'Will he have tea or coffee?' She was referring to me. Why not ask me directly? I thought that was terribly rude. Did she think I was mentally subnormal and incapable of answering for myself just because my walking was a bit funny and I twitched a lot?

'C-coffee,' I told her, annoyed with myself for stammering.

She wouldn't meet my eye; she just scribbled it down on her pad and hurried away. She definitely wasn't getting a tip, I decided angrily.

After that I became very self-conscious when we were out in public, noticing the way people would glance at me then look away again quickly, worried that they might be caught staring. Did I really look so bad? To me, I looked the same in the mirror as I always had, but the twitches were intensely annoying.

Sometimes we were taken to the theatre, but I had no patience with anything that didn't contribute directly to me being cured. Sod the Shakespeare, I thought. Just make me well and get me back to work. And hurry up about it!

CHAPTER SIX

Sandra

Headley Court was a military establishment, where they all wore uniform and you needed a pass to get through the gates. The furniture in the day rooms was standard issue, exactly the same as they put in the married persons' accommodation. The staff all seemed very nice, though, and I thought the facilities were excellent.

It was our eighth wedding anniversary, 5 November 1991, when Allen was admitted there. The first thing they did was run a series of psychometric tests to establish his brain capacity at the time. I remember one of the tests was to see whether he could put some cards into a particular sequence. The doctors told me that he would start to do it, then forget what he was doing and have to ask them to remind him. That was a bad sign, they said. It would have been better if he had laid the cards out and maybe got the sequence slightly wrong, because that would have shown that at least he understood and remembered the instruction.

They showed him a card with a shape on it and asked him what it would look like if you turned it through 90 degrees. He had no idea. They also asked him questions such as, 'If you were in a shop paying for something that cost fifty pence and you handed over a pound, how much change would you get?' And he didn't have a clue. Not a clue. I was horrified when they told me. What on earth had happened to him? Liam could have answered some of the questions he was getting wrong. They got him into intensive physio to try and deal with the twitches and loss of leg control, and speech therapy to deal with his stuttering and difficulty in forming words, but what were they going to do about his loss of cognitive powers, I wondered? How could they ever fix that? Sometimes the brain can heal, but I was aware that brain injuries can also get worse over time as more brain tissue dies off.

The extent of his brain damage sank in gradually over weeks and months, rather than straight away. When he came home for weekends, I watched him like a hawk, straining to find any glimpses of the old Allen and the relationship we used to have, hoping and praying that any day now he would snap out of it and get back to normal.

'Do you want to watch TV?' I'd ask. 'That programme you like is on.'

'OK.' He'd shrug, and we'd sit down to watch it together, but when I glanced at his face it would be blank and I could tell he wasn't following it at all. He didn't laugh at funny moments, or react in any way to what was happening on the screen.

When I referred to things we'd done together in the past, or places we'd been, there was a similar blankness. One day I pointed out our wedding photograph on the wall.

'You remember our wedding day, don't you?' There was no recognition on Allen's face. 'In Wilton?' I continued, tears coming to my eyes. 'It was Guy Fawkes Night. Your friend Kevin was best man. Look, there he is.' I pointed to the photo again.

Allen shook his head. 'Don't remember.'

'Do you remember how we met?' I persisted. He paused and then shook his head.

There had been plenty of clues before but it was then I finally realized that he didn't remember me at all from before the accident. I burst out crying, covered my face and ran upstairs. I threw myself on the bed, sobbing my heart out. I suppose I must have known already, but I hadn't wanted to admit it to myself. I wished I hadn't pushed him. It had been easier not knowing because now I had to think about all the implications of it. If he didn't remember me, did I really still have a husband?

That first day when I picked him up from Haslar he hadn't had a clue who I was. The staff had told him I was his wife, so he knew that much but no more. What if they'd made a mistake? He would probably have gone off with anyone if they told him to. The wrong woman could easily have claimed him.

It made me feel grief-stricken and terribly lonely. It was like a particularly cruel type of bereavement because I no longer had a partner who loved me although someone who looked exactly the same as him was sitting downstairs. Not four months before we'd had a lovely, romantic time visiting the sights of Penang and Singapore – the temples, the markets, the huge Buddha statues, the beaches – and we'd been a proper couple who loved each other. And now I'd lost that love and I didn't know when – or if – I would ever get it back again. Meanwhile I was burdened with someone with whom I couldn't even have a logical conversation, who needed me to be a nurse and carer and had nothing to offer in return.

He arrived on Friday evenings, sat down on a chair in the corner and hardly moved until it was time to go back on the Sunday. I tried to chat to him about what had happened during the week, about the news on TV, about the children, but I got monosyllabic responses. He only spoke when he wanted something from me: food or drink, or for the children to stop being so noisy.

It was very hard to explain to them why their daddy was so different from the fun, playful daddy they remembered. I just kept the story simple: he'd had an accident and hurt his head; he needed peace and quiet for it to get better again; they had to be careful not to bother him. They seemed to take it at face value. He was still their daddy, even if he was a bit grumpy and didn't get down on the floor to play Lego as he used to.

Every now and again I would try to set up a game that we could all play together, but Allen had no interest. He wasn't really capable of much.

'Do you want to play ball with us?' I asked once, thinking that he might be able to do throwing and catching with the kids without too much effort while sitting in a chair – but I soon realized that was another skill he had lost. When I threw the ball, he didn't have the instinct to raise his arms and catch it so it bounced off his chest. I was throwing it *at* him instead of *to* him.

After a while the children tended to give him a wide berth in case he shouted at them, or tried to grab them for a hug and squeezed too hard, misjudging his own strength.

There wasn't a big community of naval wives round our way. Army wives all live together on the base and entire regiments are moved at the same time so they are very close and able to support each other in times of trouble. In the Navy, families live off the base and are moved around one by one so you don't get to know each other in the same way. However, my wonderful next-door neighbours Julie and Heather or another friend Judy would have the children any time I asked and that was a godsend.

I called Allen's mum, of course, and his sister Suzanne, but they had their own lives to lead and couldn't be much help with his care. I later found out that his mum was struggling with the early stages of MS round about the time Allen was first back in hospital in the UK, so that might explain why she didn't often come to visit him. Maybe the drive would have been too much for her. I was the one who had to take responsibility, along with the staff at Headley Court, and that's just the way it was.

Even though I didn't have a job I was rushing around at full stretch, looking after the children during the week, running the house and buying in food so that everything was calm and ordered when Allen got back at the weekend. He didn't like to see mess or disorder.

I remember I watched news footage of uninjured soldiers returning from the Gulf with smiles from ear to ear, kissing their wives and picking up their children, and I wondered if their lives would go back to normal. I was yearning for my husband and my old life but at the same time I was beginning to lose hope that things would ever go back to the way they used to be.

About two months after the accident, I found out that Allen's salary had been stopped. I didn't realize at first because it was paid into his personal bank account, then a direct debit came across to my account to pay for household bills, rent, food and so forth. Most naval wives operate this way. You can't have joint accounts in case a situation arises where you need a joint signature for something while your husband is away at sea for months. When his income was stopped, the direct debit kept coming but I found out from statements that his account was getting seriously overdrawn.

I rang *Collingwood* naval base to request his pay slips and found that he had only been paid for the first two weeks of August. His income had been stopped on the 16th, the day he was injured, because when he went into hospital he wasn't attached to a ship or a base so he wasn't clocked as being at work. It seemed intolerable that on top of my anxiety about Allen's injury I had to worry about money as well. I ranted and raved to the authorities at *Collingwood* until eventually, a couple of months after the accident, they sorted out the problems and got him back on the payroll, although minus the extra supplement he had been getting for being at sea. It was stressful but in a way I was glad to have something practical to keep me occupied since it seemed there was nothing I could do for Allen at the time. Everywhere I turned, I hit a brick wall.

Those early weeks and months are like a thick fog and I didn't feel I was coping at all. I was frightened and vulnerable but I was angry as well and I suppose that drove me. First of all I was determined to find out exactly what had happened to Allen and see if there would be any kind of compensation for the injuries he'd suffered to help us pay for his care in the future. I consulted a lawyer, who wrote to the captain of Allen's ship.

A reply came on 1 November and it was only then I found out how the accident had happened and that he hadn't been on some unauthorized 'jolly', as had been implied at first.

Ex-pats who lived in the countries bordering the Gulf liked to entertain service personnel when they pulled into port. I remember Allen mentioning this before. He'd said that none of them were especially keen on those evenings, when conversation could be an effort, but it was considered good PR to go along. On 16 August his ship was moored in Muscat in the Gulf of Oman. Some ex-pats issued an invitation for two men to come to dinner and I'm not sure whether Allen was volunteered in his absence or if he just didn't step back quickly enough to avoid it, but he ended up being pressganged into it, along with another Chief Petty Officer.

The ex-pats picked them up from the ship in a four-wheel drive. The captain didn't know precisely what happened, but it seems that there was an accident, the car overturned and Allen's head slammed at high speed into the roof. He said that after the accident the driver had made every effort to make sure Allen was all right and had taken him back to the ship, from where he was transferred to hospital. However, he said, no one could recall the names or address of the ex-pats he had been visiting so we couldn't contact them to try and claim compensation through their insurance company.

The captain enclosed a statement from the man who had been with Allen in the car, saying that the driver had been driving with the utmost care and attention, although he couldn't say for sure whether there had been seatbelts or not. Certainly Allen hadn't been wearing one. If it turned out that there hadn't been any fitted, that could have given us possible grounds to sue for negligence.

Allen was taken to hospital in Muscat, the captain continued, but X-rays didn't show any damage to his skull or spine so they released him back to the ship. They sailed from Muscat but his condition deteriorated. Seemingly he kept trying to get out of bed and go back to his duties but he was obviously unable to work. When the ship pulled into Dubai he was admitted to hospital there, then he was placed in a hotel room under the care of the British Embassy for a week. He was brought back on board ship on the 31st, still very poorly, and on 7 September, three weeks after the accident, they arranged to medevac him back to the UK, where he was admitted to Haslar Royal Naval Hospital in Gosport, Hampshire.

My lawyer concluded that there would be a lot of obstacles to surmount if we wanted to take legal action for compensation. First, we'd have to find out who the driver was, and no one seemed to know. Next, we would have to prove negligence, and that could be tricky to do abroad, depending on the law in Oman. It was unlikely that we would have any claim against the Navy for allowing the trip to take place. And he said that the Navy would be able to refute any suggestion that lack of appropriate medical attention after the accident had contributed to Allen's condition. So it wasn't very hopeful.

In February 1992 I got another letter from the captain suggesting that it could be damaging to the Navy's relations with the ex-pat communities in the Gulf if I continued to pursue a claim. I knew I couldn't take on the might of the Royal Navy. If they weren't going to help me to track down the driver, we had to accept the fact that Allen wasn't going to get any compensation for his injuries. It felt particularly unfair because if he had tripped over a broken paving stone in Portsmouth high street, we could have got compensation. We could really have used the money to help adapt our house and make it easier for me to look after Allen there, or to pay for carers to help me when he was at home at the weekends. But the Navy had closed ranks and I knew I couldn't go any further without their help. We just had to focus on getting him better again.

When the ship he'd been on came back in to dock at Portsmouth, I went down to pick up his kit and I managed to have a chat with some friends of his in the mess. They were really upset to hear how bad his injuries were because at the time it hadn't seemed so bad.

'I thought he was OK when he first got back to the ship, apart from complaining about headaches,' one man told me. 'The first time I noticed anything peculiar was after he had been ashore in Dubai. When he came on board again, his speech was slurred and he was stammering.'

'Yeah, he didn't recognize us when he came back on board after Dubai. He seemed very confused.'

Head injuries can be like that. After a severe blow to the brain, the patient can get better or he can get progressively worse, as there may be internal bleeding or swelling that gradually kills off more and more healthy brain tissue. If you break a leg you can repair it. You might have a slight limp for a while, but with head injuries no one can tell what the prognosis is, the brain is such a complex thing.

'I'm really sorry,' they all said to me. 'Is there anything we can do?'

'Can you remember the name of the people he was visiting?' I pleaded, but they looked blank. Nobody knew.

I didn't feel any animosity towards the ex-pats. Car accidents happen. But if their insurance company had been able to pay us some money to help get Allen the best possible care and to compensate for his loss of earning power, I would have pursued that all the way.

As I was leaving the ship, someone came running after me. 'I don't suppose you could do us a favour and take Allen's medical records up to Headley Court, could you?'

'Of course,' I said. Never give a nurse some notes to transfer, especially when they aren't sealed! My first stop was a café in Portsmouth where I sat down to read through the bare bones of the story, with tears trickling down my cheeks.

Involved in RTA in Muscat, seen on ship first ... Admitted to hospital with headache, amnesia, severe neck pain, vomiting. Cervical spine and bony skull X-rays normal ... Discharge to ship on 19th. Condition remained poor with residual headache, vomiting and memory deficit, poor concentration ... Unable to restrain him on bed rest, disorientated and wandering.

Nowadays he would have been given a CT or MRI scan on admission to hospital but these things weren't routinely available back in 1991. If they'd detected pressure on the brain they'd drill boreholes to relieve it. I'll never know if this would have helped Allen or not, and there's no point in dwelling on it.

Admitted to Al-Rashid Hospital in Dubai where he was given strong analgesia ... Felt he was improved. Discharged on 24th to go on sick leave in a hotel under the care of the British Embassy ... Ship came back on 31st ... Condition stable but with severe headaches, poor concentration, neck pain, unable to perform any duties. Could take some length of time to recover.

The notes finished by recommending that he should go back to the UK for assessment and physiotherapy. They said, 'Unfortunately he is a key maintainer,' and asked for a rapid estimate of the time it would take to get him back to his post. Basically, if he was going to be 'downgraded' for more than three weeks they would need an urgent replacement because he was crucial to the functioning of the ship.

Three weeks! By this stage it was several months since he'd returned and as far as I could see nothing was going to happen fast. I couldn't think about the future though. Somehow I had to keep dragging myself through each day and trying not to break down.

It was a bad day when I read those notes. I just felt so desperately sorry for Allen – and for all of us who loved him.

CHAPTER SEVEN

Allen

As time went by and I realized that nothing was happening fast, I wanted to march out of Headley Court with my uniform and kit bag and get straight back on to a ship. In my frustration I began to rebel against the system. There was a bar for the RAF NCOs there, and Dave, the guy who was better than me at remembering the newspaper stories in the morning, started taking me there for a few pints. Once I got over my jealousy we got on brilliantly and we got ratted together more than once. The Sister gave us a telling off when we got back to the ward.

'Do you really think that's helping your condition, Dolly?'

Of course I knew it wasn't, but it helped me to let my hair down with someone who was in much the same position as myself. Dave had a black sense of humour and we were great at making fun of ourselves and our fellow patients.

'If you had five of us in a room and one left,' he joked, 'the rest of us could spend an entire morning trying to guess who had gone.'

It may not sound funny now – maybe you had to be there – but I recall my stomach aching from laughing. We'd laugh so much over the silliest things that we could hardly catch our breath.

It felt good to realize that even without the power of fluent speech, I could still make friends. All through my career, I'd got on well with everyone. I don't think anyone ever had a word to say against me. On every single ship there had been a great bunch of lads and we'd all bonded through the course of the voyage, whether it was six months or two years. It was hard to leave and move on to another ship with a different crew, but before long I'd have made a new set of friends. And I met all sorts of people when I went onshore. In America, I was hitchhiking up to LA and a chap picked me up and when he heard I didn't have anywhere to stay, he said I could borrow his girl-friend's flat for a couple of days even though he didn't know me from Adam! I think the naval uniform helped to win trust, but I suppose I must have been quite a convincing talker as well.

So when Dave and I made friends at Headley Court and started having our mad drinking nights out together, it felt as though I was getting just a little piece of normality back, and regaining a skill that I could remember I used to have in the past.

Every Friday evening, Sandra would drive the hour and a half from Emsworth to Headley Court to pick me up and take me home for the weekend. In theory I knew this was a good thing. I knew what a wife was and I knew what children were, and that going home was supposed to be nice. But in fact more than anything the weekend trips made me anxious.

Headley Court was kitted out for people recovering from injury, so they had walk-in showers and everything was easy to access. All the other men there were in the same boat as me and we had a sense of camaraderie, of struggling together. I liked my routines in Headley Court, when I knew what would be happening from one minute to the next. There was no structure to the days at home. Being there seemed to underline for me everything that I couldn't do. Everywhere I turned there were reminders of this mythical perfect husband called Allen who Sandra claimed I used to be but whom I couldn't remember.

The occupational therapists had taught me how to make a cup of tea or coffee by lifting the kettle and pouring with painstaking precision. The physio was helping me to control my twitching, so it made manual tasks easier. But when I tried to help Sandra by taking some cakes out of the oven, I forgot to wear oven gloves and burned my hand badly. I still didn't have any feeling in the right side of my body, so I didn't touch the scorching tray and jump back, the way anyone else would have, and the result was some very nasty blisters.

I tried to help by putting dishes away in the cupboards after they'd been washed, but for some reason I always put the cutlery in the wrong compartments. It's a silly thing but I think it really got on Sandra's nerves. I could see that spoons were on the left, forks in the middle and knives on the right, but when I went to put in a fork, it would go in the spoon compartment and I just wouldn't notice. It was like a complete mental blank.

I got irritated with Sandra as well. When she sat and tried to make conversation with me, I'd snap out one-word answers. I knew she was trying to tiptoe around me and keep everything light and cheerful, but somehow that made things worse. The nicer and more reasonable she tried to be, the more I snapped at her and found excuses to pick an argument.

Why hadn't the post been brought to me the second it came through the letterbox? In the Navy post was very important and when a helicopter brought your post out to the ship it was a significant moment and you dropped everything to deal with it. She explained that more likely than not the post would be for her or the kids, but I was furious that it didn't come to me first. I was the man of the house, after all.

I fixated on silly things like this and niggled at Sandra. I saw the world in black and white, truth or lies, right or wrong, with no halfway measures. Something was either hot or it was cold; I couldn't envisage the concept of 'warm'.

As over the months my frustration mounted, I began to come up with strategies to try and convince the doctors that I was getting better. I knew I wouldn't be allowed back on to active service unless my eyesight improved, so one day, before a routine eye test, I put on a pair of jeans that had holes ripped in them – a fashionable thing in those days. I sneaked into the examining room and copied the letters from the eye test on to my leg, through a hole in the jeans, because I could see pretty well close up but distance gave me problems. During the test, I read along the chart and when it reached the letters I could-n't make out I just glanced down at my knee, shifting the denim surreptitiously until I could see the next letters.

'That's brilliant, Allen!' the doctor exclaimed. 'You couldn't read that line before. Well done!'

I came up with tricks to hide my memory lapses. When they asked what I had had for breakfast, I always said, 'Toast and marmalade.' I don't know if that was true or not but if I said it with enough confidence I seemed to get away with it.

One Sunday when Sandra brought me back from a trip home, she mentioned to the doctor that we'd been out for a meal.

'What did you have to eat, Allen?' he asked.

Quick as a flash, I replied, 'Chicken curry.'

Sandra frowned at me but I ignored her. She could see through all the tricks I was playing. She knew that when a waiter read out a list of dishes, or even when I read a menu, I would only remember the last one I heard or read, so that tended to be the dish I chose. She knew that when someone asked me a question and I didn't know the answer, I would tell plausible lies rather than say, 'I don't know.' I often responded 'chicken curry' when asked about meals out, because it was the kind of thing you got on most pub menus round our way. Only Sandra knew I was faking and pretending that I was a lot better than I really was.

The hope was all in my head. The doctors had never offered me hope that I would make a full recovery. That's something I just had to accept, but I convinced myself that I'd be back on a ship before long, or in the very worst-case scenario I'd be working at a desk job. I'd fooled them with the eyesight test, and there were distinct improvements in my speech, so now I just had to overcome the memory problems.

I had fragments of images in my brain that didn't make sense on their own, like a huge jigsaw puzzle spread out on the floor with most of the pieces missing. Sometimes I thought I could remember lying on the kerb straight after the accident but I could never tell if I was just imagining that because I'd been told I was in a car at the time. I'd get intense flashbacks but I had no way of assessing where they fitted in the whole spectrum of time or place. Once I thought I had a flashback to when I was serving on HMS *Ark Royal* and I could remember the helicopters swooshing in to land on deck. I told a few people about it, delighted to have recovered another memory, but then Sandra overheard me.

'Sorry, Allen,' she said, 'but you were never on the *Ark Royal*.'

I'd been hoping that if I had enough flashbacks one day they would all join up together and the memories would make sense, but if they were unreliable, it was another setback.

'If you sit and worry about what you've forgotten, you've wasted a day,' a doctor told me. 'You won't ever miraculously rebuild the part of your brain that is damaged, but it's quite an amazing organ and it can learn to reroute things through undamaged areas.'

I clung to any germ of positive feedback and ignored the negative. I just didn't accept that my reduced cognitive powers were going to make it impossible for me to go back to my old job. Like an alcoholic, I was in denial about the scale of my disabilities. Everyone else had a problem, not me. They were wrong and I was right and that's all there was to it.

CHAPTER EIGHT

Sandra

I cried a lot in those early days. I felt like a widow with two young children to bring up, yet every weekend I had the additional responsibility of caring for a hostile, sullen, incapacitated man who inhabited my husband's body. I could easily have sunk into despair, but a survival mechanism kicked in and I started analysing Allen's capabilities as closely as I could to try and work out what was going on and what help he needed. We would try everything possible, no matter what it took.

Some of his symptoms reminded me of stroke patients I'd worked with. He had a mixture of numbness and pins and needles down his right side, so he could hold a cup with his right hand but he couldn't tell you if it was hot or cold. A few times he burned himself touching something that was scalding. He had no sense of danger, so if I said to him: 'Watch out

– the cooker's on!' he'd put out his hand to touch the rings and see which one was hot. If we went outside, he'd step straight into the road without checking to see if there was any traffic coming.

Allen often got confused and thought he was still on the ship, so he yelled at me for storing the ironing board vertically. On board you always lay it flat on the floor so it doesn't fall over with the movement of the vessel. And he went mad if the post wasn't brought to him straight away, because that's what would happen on a ship.

He could dress himself in the morning but he often got things back to front or inside out and he became very irritable if I pointed out that his shirt was the wrong way round or his socks didn't match. He'd glare at me sometimes with a mixture of rage and hatred, as if what had happened was all my fault. Most of the time he sat in a chair in the corner of the sitting room ignoring us all, sulking in his own little world.

His memory for words was poor but he would try to describe what he wanted and I had to guess. I remember once he said to me to put his sandwich 'on the thing … top … legs'.

'Do you mean the table?' I asked and he nodded, annoyed with himself. I felt sorry for him then. How frustrating it must be not to remember a basic word like 'table'. I could see it drove him nuts.

Sometimes he would get part of the way through a sentence and stop. I would ask, 'And?' He'd snap, 'I wasn't talking.' He'd forgotten already. His memory was just appalling.

The staff at Headley Court gave him a notebook in which he could write down things he needed to remember, so I'd be talking to him about something and suddenly he'd take out this book from his pocket and start scribbling. When I sneaked a look later, I found that his writing was very poor. A lot of it was back to front and it was all in capitals, and the words frequently didn't make any sense. I'm not sure if he ever read it back but I can't imagine it was much use to him. I showed a sample of his writing to a special needs teacher at the kids' school and she said it looked like a classic case of acquired dyslexia.

The speech therapists tried to get him to speak slowly rather than rushing headlong, but that just meant he was even more likely to forget what he was talking about before he got to the end of his sentence. He wasn't a big fan of those therapists, but I thought they were doing a good job because I started to see a difference in the clarity of his speech quite quickly.

However, the more clearly he could speak, the more he could argue with me. Some weekends I couldn't do a thing right and I faced streams of criticism from the moment I arrived to pick him up: I was late, I hadn't brought him something he'd asked for, or I spent too long chatting to the nurses when he wanted to leave. Back at home, he would criticize anything and everything: the meals I made weren't right, I hadn't ironed the shirt he wanted and, most frequently, the children were too noisy.

I tried my best to stay positive when he was around and not to engage in arguments, but I could sense his frustration mounting. He was angry a lot of the time because of his lapses of memory, and he got angry with me because there was no one else he could take it out on. I don't think he would have dreamed of being quite so rude to the staff at Headley Court because they would have told him where to get off.

We still got invitations to events at the naval base in Portsmouth and about six months after the accident I decided I would take Allen along to the Valentine's Dinner. Maybe part of his frustration stemmed from boredom. It might be good for him to see some old friends and familiar surroundings, I reckoned, and at the very least we were guaranteed a good meal.

I soon wished we hadn't gone though. I wasn't ready for the hush as we walked into the room and everyone saw how difficult it was for Allen to walk with his rolling, loping gait and his persistent twitching. He would never let me bring a wheelchair to help him get around; he had to do it himself. There's a photo of us taken at the event and they've propped Allen up against a mantelpiece but you can tell that he's not supporting himself very well. If the mantelpiece hadn't been there, he'd have fallen flat on his face.

Naval dinners are very formal affairs, with a corsage for the ladies, silver service and all sorts of toasts and traditions. People rushed to open doors for Allen and me and they waved hello, but they were too embarrassed to come over and engage in conversation. I felt they were avoiding us, just as some people might avoid the old lady in the village who's lost her husband for fear they will get dragged into hearing about her loneliness. I was lonely during the pre-dinner drinks and the meal, because there was no one for me to talk to. Allen was silent and scowling, just focusing on eating his dinner and not making eye contact with anyone, least of all me.

He used to have beautiful manners in the old days, always introducing me to everyone, pulling out my chair for me and keeping my glass topped up. Now he was too insular to think of anyone else but himself. His table manners had slipped as well, I noted, as he shovelled food into his mouth without waiting till other people at the table had been served. It was all so unlike him.

After the dinner there was dancing, and several officers came over to ask me to dance but I knew it was out of pity.

'Someone look after Parton's wife,' they'd be saying to each other, and a volunteer would roll up in front of me offering his hand.

I couldn't wait to make our excuses and leave, and I decided I wouldn't put myself through that again in a hurry. I didn't want to be an object of pity and I didn't want Allen to be one either.

At Headley Court, Allen fell in with a bunch of lads who could be a bit badly behaved, and they all covered for each other in front of the staff. The ones who didn't have brain injuries could go out into the local town and pick up booze or whatever the rest of them needed. They'd pool the chores, so that the ones with arms but no legs could do the washing-up, the ones who were good at craft helped the others with the projects they'd been assigned by the occupational therapists, and the ones with better memories reminded the others of things they needed to do. Some of the staff thought they were a bit disruptive, but Allen always liked being part of a fun group of lads so on the whole I decided it was probably good for his morale.

What I approved less of was him trying to pull a fast one and convince the staff that his memory was improving when in my opinion it was actually getting worse.

'We think he's getting better,' a nurse said to me, 'because he was able to tell us what he had for breakfast when he was back at yours for the weekend.'

'What did he say?'

'Bacon sandwiches.' She looked at me questioningly. 'Is that right?'

'Well, the truth is that Allen never eats breakfast and he certainly didn't have bacon this weekend because I don't have any in the house.'

And I knew his trick of always ordering chicken curry so that when they came round and said: 'Who ordered the chicken curry?' he would remember it was him. Otherwise he would have had no idea. I wished with all my heart it was true that he was improving, but genuinely I didn't see it when he came home at the weekends. He wasn't a 'vegetable' by any means. He'd been an extremely intelligent man before the accident and the basic intelligence was still in there, but without memory it's not much use.

His sense of humour had also disappeared, certainly for the first year after the accident, and his illness made him very selfish. He had never been selfish before. The man I'd married was generous and considerate. He didn't realize he was being selfish but he seemed to have lost any ability to think about how his actions might affect me or the kids. This man was like an irritable stranger to us.

It was a very difficult time: very sad and very difficult; I missed the old Allen so badly that it hurt physically. I had an aching in my chest a lot of the time. When I thought back to all the ways he used to solve problems for me and help me to cope with difficulties, tears would spring to my eyes. But I couldn't give in to them. He'd looked after me before when I was struggling to cope with my second pregnancy, and now it was my turn to be there for him. I had to stay strong for Allen and see what could be done for him.

CHAPTER NINE

Allen

I might have found it difficult spending weekends at home with Sandra and the kids, but I quickly came to rely on them as part of my new life. I'd have my bag packed from lunchtime on Friday and would be watching the clock for this woman. I may not have any memories of her from before I was injured, but I knew she was always kind and gentle with me. Her house was comfortable and the food was good. I could turn on the television without arguing with half a dozen other guys about which channel we should watch. And if the children drove me crazy sometimes with their noise and boisterousness, I liked the way they just accepted me as I was and didn't talk down to me or treat me like a basket case. Their dad had a few problems but he was still their dad.

One Friday afternoon in Headley Court, a nurse came to see me. 'I'm afraid I've got bad news, Allen. Your wife is ill this weekend and isn't going to be able to come and get you.'

I took this in, then blurted: 'Taxi!' Surely they could find a way to send me back home without Sandra having to pick me up?

'It's not a good idea for you to go there. She's got flu and we don't want you to catch it and bring it back to the other men. I'm sorry, Allen, but you're stuck with us for the weekend this time.'

My bag was already packed and sitting on my bed. I went into the dorm and looked at it and thought to myself: This won't do. I'm not accepting this. If Sandra wasn't coming to get me, I would make my own way to her.

However, in my befuddled brain I remembered the married quarters we used to live in when we were at Rosyth and I confused it with another memory of a journey to Glasgow I used to make four times a week from Bath, when I was working at the underground base there. We didn't have email back then, so I would have to fly up and down collecting services data and bringing it back with me, and the details of that journey were still clear in my mind. I used to have dozens of open shuttle tickets and I just walked on and off the planes as if they were buses.

Sandra had brought my bag back from the ship. I dragged it out, opened it and started rifling through the contents. In a folder at the bottom I found what I was looking for – an unused open shuttle ticket – and I stuck it in my jacket pocket.

I joined a coach party of patients who were leaving Headley Court on their way to a day out in Leatherhead. From there I somehow managed to get myself to Heathrow airport, although I've got no idea how. I produced my plane ticket, got on a flight to Glasgow, and at the other end I climbed in a taxi and ended up in a pub I knew in the city centre, which used to be the RAF club up there. I don't remember any of this now and I've got no idea how I managed it with my very limited speech. All I know is what I've heard from Sandra and the staff at Headley Court.

Seemingly I was sitting in the pub with no shirt on – I've got no idea why, but maybe I was too hot. A lovely Scottish couple who knew me from before the accident came up to have a chat. They soon realized I wasn't the full sherbet and they had a look in my wallet, where they found Sandra's number and rang her.

'We're with Dolly,' they said. 'Do you know him?'

'Ye-es,' she answered cautiously.

'Well, Dolly's in the pub with us and we're really worried about him. He doesn't seem right.'

'Which pub?' Sandra asked, assuming it must be one somewhere in the vicinity of Headley Court.

'It's the Arlington,' they told her. 'In Woodlands Road.'

'Which town?' she asked, not recognizing the street name.

She couldn't believe her ears when they said Glasgow. Surely it couldn't be her husband all the way up there? She took a note of the phone number of the pub and said she would call them back shortly, and then she rang the ward at Headley Court.

'Is Allen there?' she asked.

'Yeah. He's … I just saw him by his bed a little while ago.' The warden went through to the dormitory to check and found that I wasn't there after all. He continued, 'Some of the men have gone on a trip to Leatherhead, so maybe he's on that. I'll check and get back to you.'

It was about ten minutes later when Headley Court realized that they had lost a neurological patient. They rang Sandra back.

'Where did you say he was?' the warden asked.

'It's a pub in Glasgow.'

'Glasgow, Scotland?' They were incredulous.

Sandra gave them the phone number and the names of the couple who had phoned her, and everyone sprang into action. It was arranged that the nuclear submarine base at Faslane, just outside Glasgow, would send an ambulance to the pub to pick me up. I believe I let them collect me without a fuss. I must have realized something had gone wrong, because my mission had been to track down Sandra and patently she wasn't there.

I wasn't supposed to fly because the cabin pressure could be bad for my brain injury so they took me up to Faslane naval base to spend the night. When I woke up in the morning, I saw the once-familiar view of submarine conning towers against the skyline, in place of the neat topiary gardens at Headley Court with their round, square and triangular-shaped trees, and I thought, Hmm, this is interesting. I'd have given anything to be back working there instead of staying the night as a runaway.

Sandra phoned to talk to me and she was very upset. She said that I had run away to punish her for not picking me up, and that it wasn't fair of me to put her under that pressure when she had so much else going on in her life. She was ill, she had financial worries, and she had the children to look after as well.

I listened, and I suppose I felt bad for upsetting her so much but one of the side effects of my brain injury was an inability to empathize with other people and put myself in their shoes. Emotionally, I was a blank canvas.

They drove me back down to Headley Court in an ambulance, at great expense to the taxpayer I suppose, and my fellow patients greeted me with whoops and cheers, although the staff were a little more frosty.

When I next saw the neurological specialist, he had a positive take on my adventure: 'I'm impressed at the cognitive abilities you displayed in getting yourself up there,' he said. 'Just don't do it again!'

After this, my campaign to convince the powers-that-be I was ready to go back to work intensified. I developed all sorts of ways of deluding people that I could remember things. Some of the group of lads helped. We pooled our skills and all helped each other. If you keep talking and sound confident about what you're saying, it usually carries people along with you. If I had seen a picture of an event I could pretend I remembered it and even recall some detail from the picture to convince the listener. Memory loss is never total; there are glimpses and hints. I still remembered all the practical things, like how to get dressed in the morning, how to shave and brush my teeth, and, of course, how to get to Glasgow. So as far as I was concerned, the rest would come back over time.

My friend Dave and I were constantly comparing symptoms and memories with each other. I suppose there was a gang of about five of us who hung around together, taking refuge in black humour and practical jokes. The staff weren't entirely approving and I got told off more times than I could remember (although in those days, that wasn't many).

Sandra became friendly with a woman whose husband was also being treated for a brain injury at Headley Court but he was allowed to drive, so we got into a routine that he would bring me home on Fridays and Sandra would bring me back on the Sunday, so she only had to do the journey once a week instead of twice. That suited me because I didn't like it when Sandra came to Headley Court and talked to the doctors. She tended to tell them things I didn't want them to know.

They had case conferences about me from time to time and all went well if I was allowed to speak on my own behalf, but I used to be aware of a change of attitude after Sandra had spoken to them. She told the doctors about the huge memory lapses and the techniques I was using to convince people I was getting better. She told them that I showed no recognition of family photos, and seemed to have no memories of her and the children. She told them that while I might pretend to use my right arm normally, I had absolutely no feeling in it. In fact, if I put my arm behind my back where I couldn't see it, it was as if I didn't have an arm at all. In my head, it didn't exist.

I started to get paranoid, and accused Sandra of snooping on me and telling tales. I wondered if they were bugging me, or if there were secret cameras watching me. I decided that I couldn't trust anyone; they were all against me, all trying to stop me getting back to work for their own ulterior motives.

I must have conveyed this paranoia to the doctor, because he said to me one day, 'I know you think people are spying on you and discussing you behind your back, but you should be aware that it is a common symptom of a brain injury to experience paranoid thoughts. I'm going to give you an extra pill to put a stop to this because it can't be very pleasant for you. You have to believe that we are all here to support you, Allen. We all want the same thing, and that's for you to get as well as you can possibly be.'

I didn't trust him. I thought he was trying to brainwash me and he would report the details of any conversations we had to my superiors in the Navy, so I kept quiet. I also started hiding my pills and not taking them if I could get away with it. I didn't want them to drug me up because then I wouldn't know whom to trust or what to believe any more. I needed to think as clearly as I could.

I didn't realize it at the time, but I was slipping further and further into a deep depression. This recovery was taking far too long. I didn't have an awareness of time but I asked

Sandra and she told me that I had been at Headley Court for four months. It was a ridiculous length of time to spend in hospital when there were ships out at sea that needed my weapons expertise. I was desperate to work again, no matter at what. Without my work, I had no sense of purpose, no reason to exist.

I pleaded desperately with the doctors to discharge me, saying I would be happy to take a menial desk job for the time being, just to prove myself, but that it was crucial I got back to work. I quoted detailed weapons maintenance schedules, trying to demonstrate that I was capable. I lost my temper and accused them of being unpatriotic. I growled at Sandra and I swore at the orderlies and nurses and the other men. More and more I was filled with hatred for everyone around me.

And then in March 1992, I suffered a major collapse. I thought I had an upset stomach at first and spent the morning in bed, and at some point I lapsed into unconsciousness. A nurse must have found me and I've heard there was a farcical scene when they couldn't get the main gates open to let an ambulance through. I think their emergency systems were reviewed after that. I don't remember what happened, though, because I was profoundly unconscious.

I woke up in a ward in the Atkinson Morley Hospital in London with a drip in my arm and a load of monitors ticking away all round me and I thought: What the hell?

When a doctor came, he explained to me that they didn't know exactly what had happened but they were running tests. I couldn't follow what he was saying, but when I tried to get out of bed to go to the toilet, I realized my legs weren't working any more and they wouldn't even support my weight. I used to be able to make them do roughly what I wanted with a huge effort of will, but now that had gone.

I sat on the bed summoning every ounce of willpower to try and move my legs but they didn't seem to be responding. What on earth was going on?

'You've had a bit of a setback,' the doctor told me. 'We're not sure what's happened but we're running tests. Your wife's on her way.'

I didn't want my wife; I wanted to be able to walk. I was utterly furious. I snapped at the nurses, and yelled at Sandra when she arrived, and something within me collapsed. I'd been managing to keep myself going by working really hard towards my goal of getting back on a ship again. I couldn't bear to take a step backwards on the journey – and it seemed as though this was a huge one.

I kept rolling myself out of bed and trying to force my legs to take my weight, but I'd end up a crumpled heap on the floor. More than once I broke down in tears of sheer frustration. It was so bloody unfair. Why me? Why should this have happened when I'd been going to a stupid ex-pat's dinner I hadn't even wanted to go to? I'd been good at my job, a decent boss, friends with the other men; none of this was fair. I wanted to shout at the top of my lungs in my rage at the universe.

A physiotherapist came to visit me bringing a wheelchair. She was just a young girl, full of false cheerfulness.

'Hi there! I've come to show you how to use a chair. Are you feeling up to it?'

'I don't want a chair!' I growled.

'It's worth learning the basics so you can use it as a back-up, if you need to.' She smiled, trying to win me over.

'Sod that! Teach me to walk again, not to be a cripple!' I snapped. 'You've got the wrong man. I refuse to be disabled. I will not use a wheelchair! Got it?'

She backed off. 'OK. I'd better have a word with the doctor then. He'll probably come and see you later.'

I spoke to umpteen doctors and nurses and physios and said the same thing to all of them. 'Don't give me your wheel-chairs. I've got two legs and there's nothing wrong with them. Just fix me up so I can walk again!'

They didn't seem to know what to do with me at the Atkinson Morley, so I was transferred somewhere else. They'd assess me, change my medication, run their own cognitive tests, and then pass me on to the next person because they couldn't think of anything more to do. I don't remember all the places I stayed, but I know I was getting more and more furious. What was the point of modern medicine if they couldn't fix me up? As far as I was concerned they were all useless.

CHAPTER TEN

Sandra

I was aware that Allen had been getting very depressed and angry, as all his plans to get out of hospital and back to work seemed to be coming to nothing. Personally I never thought about the future. I just kept going from one week to the next and did what needed to be done, but Allen was getting fed up with doing his physio and his speech therapy and his newspaper group every morning, and feeling as though he was on a treadmill. He was working as hard as he could and not moving forward at all.

And then late one evening I got a call from Headley Court to say he'd collapsed and was being sent to Epsom hospital.

'Don't worry!' they said – but I was frantic. I knew they wouldn't send him to hospital unless they thought there had been a deterioration in his brain condition. I probed further and was told that he had had an upset stomach and had been in bed all day; later, when a nurse tried to rouse him, he wouldn't waken. He was unconscious. That wasn't good. Basically, the longer you are unconscious, the worse the prognosis.

'Will you phone me as soon as there's any more news?' I asked. 'I mean anything at all?'

They promised they'd call if there were any changes overnight. At the time we didn't have a telephone upstairs in our house and I was worried that I wouldn't hear it ringing if I went to bed. But if I slept downstairs, I wouldn't be able to hear if the children called out and needed anything in the night. In the end, I pulled the phone as far up the stairs as the flex would go, then went and lay on my bed with the door open, but I didn't get any sleep anyway.

At seven in the morning when I hadn't heard anything, I rang the hospital and they said he'd been transferred to the Atkinson Morley in London in the middle of the night. I was furious that I hadn't been told. When I called there, they said please could I go up as soon as possible. I didn't ask why. I just made a few phone calls to get someone to look after the kids and off I went.

I could feel all the old panic-attack symptoms I used to get when I had post-natal depression – breathlessness, sweaty palms, tight chest – but I couldn't afford to give in to them. I had to get on a train up to London to be with my husband. I'd been taught some techniques for dealing with panic attacks and I used them all now. I chose a seat by an open window so there was a light breeze blowing on my face to stop me feeling faint; I made sure I was near a door in case I needed to get off in a hurry; and I cupped my hands and breathed into them because that helps to stop you getting dizzy when you are overbreathing. I don't know what the other passengers thought of me, but somehow I got there in one piece.

A doctor saw me straight away, and what he had to say was very interesting. This was the first time that a civilian doctor had assessed Allen's condition, and he said first of all that while Allen had regained consciousness he was very confused and he seemed to have lost control of his legs. There was marked right-sided hemiplegia. The physical brain damage they could detect in CT scans didn't seem to account for the extent of the disability he was suffering, and in their opinion there could be something more to it. He said that the symptoms he was experiencing were similar to those he would expect to see in someone who had been poisoned in some way, and because he knew Allen had been in the Gulf War he wondered if he might have been exposed to depleted uranium.

I said it was entirely possible he'd been exposed to depleted uranium, since he had been working with naval weapons systems for most of his career. I remember worrying once when he described to me the way that a cloud of uranium dust would waft back down the sides of the ship after they'd been firing rounds at the front. I warned him to try and stay clear of it but he said they had to be out on deck to see what was going on. 'Besides,' he added, 'you haven't noticed me glowing in the dark yet, have you?'

Another theory was lead poisoning, since it interferes with brain function, and they wanted my permission to test for both.

I agreed straight away. I'd have tried anything if I thought it had a chance of helping. I was always reading medical journals and health magazines looking for ideas or remedies we could try, so it was good to see a new specialist considering Allen's case afresh and coming up with theories that might help lead to, if not a cure, maybe a more successful form of treatment.

But any optimism I might have felt disappeared when I was taken to see him. I could tell straight away that he had taken a serious turn for the worse. He was very confused, didn't know where he was and seemed much more ill than when I had last seen him a few days earlier. When he wanted to get out of bed to go to the toilet he couldn't support his weight on his legs any more, so I had to help him into a wheelchair and push him there. He didn't want to get in it but he had no other way of getting to the loo.

The staff told me he was refusing to learn how to use a wheelchair but that there was no alternative now. Almost overnight there had been a marked deterioration in his speech, balance, walking and memory. It was utterly depressing for me and I can't begin to imagine how devastating it was for him.

The physical tests they did at the Atkinson Morley came back inconclusive but no one pursued the depleted-uranium or lead-poisoning theories any further because after a couple of weeks he was moved to yet another hospital. During 1992 he was in half a dozen different hospitals for tests and assessments and none of them seemed to get us any further. I found that his notes didn't always follow him from one hospital to the next, so I asked if I could make copies whenever possible so that I could show them to the next lot of doctors and nurses. At least that way there would be some kind of continuity in his care despite the frequent changes of location. I knew the doctors didn't always tell me everything, but I didn't find out anything I didn't know already from those notes. They just listed the care he was receiving rather than giving a complete overview or any kind of prognosis.

I had other worries on my mind at the time. Financially things were tight and I was arguing with the Navy that, on top of Allen's basic salary, we were entitled to separation allowance since we were obviously separated. This was a supplement they usually paid when he was away on a ship, but I felt we should be entitled to it just now since we weren't living apart through choice. On top of that, it was actually costing me money to go and visit him in all the different hospitals and I argued that they should help out a bit more with my travel expenses. All of this took energy, though, and some days I woke up so depressed that I could barely get the kids to school.

On the good days, I was still trying to brainstorm new ideas to help Allen. The Navy had been his whole life and I began to wonder if giving him a chance to get back to work might trigger something in his brain, the way tapes of loved ones' voices or favourite pieces of music can help to bring people out of comas. It was certainly worth a try. All the doctors had tried out their pet theories and none of them had worked.

I started talking to anyone who would listen about finding some kind of meaningful occupation for him that would make him feel like a useful member of society again. The crafts he did at Headley Court – like making pictures from bits of string wound round nails – were soul-destroying for someone with his intelligence and career history. I said that unless Allen could find something to do with his life, he would crack up completely. Personally I couldn't think of anything else to try, so I was delighted when they agreed he could do some work experience at HMS *Collingwood*.

At last things were beginning to look slightly more positive, even if I felt as though I was on a giant emotional seesaw. Allen came back to live at home, from where he would be bussed to work every day. It seemed as though things might be looking up – but not for long.

CHAPTER ELEVEN

Allen

Someone suggested that I be given a job at HMS *Collingwood* for a while on a trial basis to see how I coped.

At last! I thought. A chance to prove that I can still do the job!

They explained that I would live at home with Sandra and the kids, and I would be picked up in a minibus every morning. It would be my responsibility to check the car passes of everyone coming on and off the base, as well as doing some other bits and pieces of copying and admin. I could use the gym and facilities at *Collingwood* and eat my lunch in the mess, then go back home in the evening.

Fantastic! No problem, I thought.

I started my new job, and never was there a more fastidious car-pass checker than I. I did everything by the rule book.

Normally if someone had lost their car pass, they would just come and ask for another one to be issued, but I filled out all the proper paperwork. That meant they were automatically reported and fined, because according to the regulations it was an offence to lose your car pass. I suppose that probably didn't make me very popular with some, but the bosses were delighted that I didn't take any shortcuts.

Another of my jobs was copying out instructions on special forms, and I was very slow but I was painstaking and made sure my letters were scrupulously neat. In the therapy groups at Headley Court I had only ever written in capitals for some reason, but these instructions had to be in lower case so it was good practice for me. I'd been working hard at my writing, because obviously I had to get it back to normal before I could go back to my old job. My eyesight had improved but it never got back to the perfect vision I'd had before the accident and I had to wear glasses for close work.

There was a fantastic sports centre with a full, Olympic-sized swimming pool where I used to go just about every day to swim a few lengths. The instructor there would sit with a cup of coffee and let me get on with it. I liked swimming, because it was good for developing upper body strength. I'd given in and was using a wheelchair whenever I had to travel any distance at all, because it was impossible to drag myself round by the arms all the time. In the water I floated easily and could pretend for a few moments that I still had the use of my legs. The difference between me and an able-bodied man wasn't quite so obvious.

I had regular appointments with a psychologist at *Colling-wood*, who tried to help me to improve my social graces and think about how others might be feeling. I still used to bark out my words and offend people without having any aware-ness that I had insulted them, and then I'd be puzzled when they stopped chatting to me.

'Have you lost weight?' I asked a woman I worked along-side.

'No,' she said, puzzled.

'I didn't think so,' I continued, without any inkling that it might sound rude.

And I couldn't seem to understand other people's emotions. When Sandra burst into tears, it went right over my head. The psychologist taught me just to put my arm around her, even if I didn't know why she was crying.

The psychologist often talked to me about coming to terms with the fact that I was confined to a wheelchair, but I resis-ted this vehemently. I didn't intend to spend the rest of my life in a wheelchair. He asked me once if I was able-bodied in my dreams.

I thought long and hard before I answered truthfully, 'I don't dream any more.'

'Are you sure?' he asked. 'Maybe you're just not remem-bering them when you wake up?'

I shook my head. 'I go to bed and I sleep.'

He told me this sometimes happened with people who have lesions in the brain and that I shouldn't worry about it, but I remember being concerned that it was one more function I had lost. He said it didn't matter, that I still had the healthy type of REM sleep, and that maybe the dreams would come back one day.

Everyone was very kind to me, but I was aware that I was being watched most of the time. The ladies in the mess were always giving me cups of coffee and dropping by to make sure I was all right. When I went to the gym, there was usually someone hanging around on the balcony up above, if not in the gym itself. Even if I sat down to watch telly in one of my breaks, someone else would sidle in to sit with me. They were mothering me. In a funny way, I was better looked after there than I was in hospital.

I enjoyed being busy again, but the longer I stayed at *Collingwood*, the more I became aware of my limitations and realized that I wasn't ready for any job more taxing than checking car passes and copying out instructions. It was incredibly frustrating, but I kept coming up against blanks in my memory, things I knew I should be able to remember but couldn't. My boss might ask me to do something, and then later he'd say, 'Did you manage to get it done?' and I'd realize it had completely slipped my mind. I started noting everything down in a little notebook to try and become more efficient, but then I would forget to look at my book, and I'd be furious with myself.

I had to use a wheelchair because of the distances I had to cover during the day, but I still swore to myself this was only temporary. First I would prove myself on the job and then I would get myself walking again. I couldn't do both at once. I was putting myself under huge pressure to succeed and I got furious if I felt anyone wasn't 100 per cent on my side. Didn't they know what had happened to me? Weren't they aware how unfair it was?

I wanted to be treated fairly and given a chance, but I'd only been working at *Collingwood* for four months when they decided I had to go back to Headley Court for a month's reassessment. I argued against it – I'd had enough doctors and hospitals to last me a lifetime – but their minds were made up.

I think the staff at Headley Court were a bit shocked at the physical and mental decline I'd experienced since they'd last seen me, and that was very depressing. Also, they seemed to be taking a psychiatric rather than a neurological view and in my opinion they were barking up the wrong tree. I chatted to an expert in post-traumatic stress disorder – the top man in the country, I'm told – but that wasn't my problem. I also had a visit from a charity called Combat Stress, but there wasn't much they could do because I hadn't been in combat and I wasn't stressed.

'There's nothing wrong with my mind,' I kept repeating every time they harped on about depression and anger and so forth. 'It's my body that needs fixing.'

I just wanted to get back to my job at *Collingwood*, but instead they decided to send me somewhere else – to a psychiatric unit at RAF Hospital Wroughton near Swindon, where they had state-of-the-art brain scanners. By that stage I had reached rock bottom. My psychological decline was the worst thing. I felt a real closing down. No one could get through to me any more. Sandra has a photograph of me from that period and I look skeletal, with dead eyes and no spark of life about me.

I felt as though I was in a huge pit of despair and it was getting deeper and darker. It made me think of films where you see someone stepping into quicksand and the more they struggle, the deeper they sink. I was ready to give up the struggle because I could sense it wasn't getting me anywhere. Then I heard that another patient had escaped from Swindon and thrown himself off a motorway bridge nearby. I didn't know him so I wasn't personally upset but maybe it acted as a kind of trigger for me. It was as if somehow it gave me permission.

I was still stashing away any pills I didn't want to take in a drawer in my bedside cabinet. I don't know how many I'd amassed but it was quite a collection. I can't remember anything except that one night, when everyone else on the ward was asleep, I quietly slid my drawer open and began swallowing the paracetamol they'd been giving me, one by one, washing them down with water. I took all the pills I had, and then I lay back on my pillows and closed my eyes, waiting to die.

CHAPTER TWELVE

Sandra

I soon realized Allen's job at *Collingwood* wasn't working out. He came home one Friday saying he'd had a really good day and proudly showed me some of the work he'd been doing, copying out records.

It may sound strange but in those days they didn't have everything computerized and sometimes a document couldn't be taken from one part of a building to another for security reasons, so they would copy out the relevant part of it. I looked at the work Allen had done and the first line was beautifully neat, with the best lettering I had seen him do since the accident, but underneath it he had copied the same first line again and again, so it said the same thing all the way down the page. I didn't know what to say to him as he stood there looking for my praise.

'Didn't you hand it in when you'd finished?' I asked.

'They said I could bring it home,' he replied, obviously not seeing anything unusual in that.

'Just do your best,' I kept urging him, in exactly the same words I used when the kids had tests at school. 'Everyone's on your side and wants you to succeed.'

I suspected his time in the job would be limited if all his work was like this and it was hard to think what they would offer him next. Sometimes people who had been injured were given jobs training new recruits; this was often what happened if they had lost their legs, for example, and couldn't be on active service on a ship any more. But I knew Allen couldn't have coped with a teaching job. His brain just wasn't up to it.

The months went by and they seemed to be doing their best to help the job work out, so I crossed my fingers and waited. But then they decided to run more psychiatric evaluations and he was transferred first to Headley Court, and then to RAF Wroughton in Swindon. There they had a theory that his memory loss and cognitive problems might be related to a traumatic event he had witnessed, possibly in the Gulf, that his mind was blocking out. They asked my permission to try hypnotherapy to see if anything surfaced, and once again I agreed. Every doctor I met in those days seemed to have a new theory or a different view but I was glad that at least they were trying.

The hypnotherapy didn't reveal anything new, though, so that was another avenue closed. I went home feeling gloomy. What would they come up with next? Where would he be sent now?

Some Navy people were fantastically helpful, and one of these was my family support worker, Isabel. She'd been an absolute rock ever since Allen was first flown home from the Gulf. When I saw her car pull up outside the house one morning while Allen was in hospital in Swindon, I thought maybe she had some news for me about my claims for more money. But it wasn't that.

'I'm afraid I've got some bad news for you, Sandra. I don't know how to tell you this, but Allen took an overdose last night. He'd got hold of a load of paracetamol from somewhere and he swallowed rather a lot of them.'

I sat down hard. 'How is he? Have they pumped his stomach?'

'He's going to pull through. They're giving him Parvalax to neutralize it. I'm so sorry.'

I opened my mouth to say something but tears started to come instead. I was so shocked. Although I knew Allen had been very depressed, I'd never thought he was the type to commit suicide. It was totally out of character for him – or at least it would have been for the old Allen, the one I had married. What had brought him to the point that he was ready to give up?

I remembered that once, when the children were still babies, I'd had a very bad headache and I'd stopped at McDonald's to buy a Coke with which to swallow some headache pills. I tipped them out of my handbag and there were only two left, and I thought: God, that's sod's law. Only two left, so even if I wanted to I couldn't take any more. My post-natal depression was at its worst and that's why the thought of suicide briefly entered my head, but I could never have done anything about it. What was so hard to understand was that Allen had actually taken that step. I knew he must have been feeling really bad to have made that choice.

I cried for days and days on end. We were all failing him. He needed help, and of all the doctors and therapists he had seen, none had been able to give him a reason to keep on living, or convince him that he had a worthwhile future. When I next visited him, I just hugged him with tear-filled eyes but we didn't talk about it. I think it's possible he had already forgotten what he had done. My impression was that it had been a spur-of-the-moment act rather than something he had been planning for ages. He felt down, he came across the pills and he took them.

They kept him at Wroughton for just over a month then discharged him and he went back to the job at *Collingwood*, but there was a continuing programme of assessments and investigations he had to go through.

In November 1992, he was told he was to be sent for some tests at Haslar hospital. One of these was for BSE, commonly known as Mad Cow Disease at the time, because they thought his persistent twitching and flailing attempts to drag himself around could be a symptom of it. The other theory was that he might have a type of encephalitis that occurs in people who are HIV positive.

I got a phone call to warn me he was having an AIDS test,

and they told me that Allen had gone berserk, throwing things round the room when he heard about it.

'How dare you question my sexuality?' he'd yelled at them.

They tried to explain that there were all sorts of ways he could have contracted HIV:

'According to your records you had several blood transfusions after breaking your leg in the early 1980s and you've had umpteen injections when travelling to foreign countries. It just takes one unsterilized needle. Nothing to do with sex.'

But Allen still refused to take the test until they told him it was a condition of him remaining in the Navy. I was very shocked and upset about the whole business, because if he was HIV positive, there was a chance the kids and I could be as well. I waited with bated breath for almost a week before I finally got a call to say that the BSE and HIV tests were both negative.

And then, just when it seemed things couldn't get any worse, I picked up the post in the morning to find some eviction papers. I had to read them several times before I could make sense of the stern, formulaic language. The Navy wanted us out of our house. My legs turned to jelly and I sat down hard on the sofa. How could they do this to us? Where were we supposed to live? Surely there had to have been a mistake?

I phoned Family Services to see what had happened and was told that after Allen was discharged from Headley Court he was no longer attached to a naval base and so was not entitled to married quarters any more. I couldn't believe my ears.

It seemed heartless in the extreme. If I had fought hard, kicking and screaming, I could maybe have got the eviction order overturned, but there was a part of me that was beginning to realize Allen didn't have a future in the Navy. If we didn't leave naval quarters now, I'd have to do so at some point a few months down the line, so I decided to explore the options. I wanted to have a support network in place for when he became a civilian again and I knew it was going to take a lot of advance planning.

I asked around and found out about a charity called Housing 21, a little-known offshoot of the British Legion that specialized in housing ex-service personnel. At first they said I couldn't apply because Allen was still in the Navy, but all the doctors and therapists I talked to said it looked increasingly likely that Allen would be discharged at some point in the near future, so Housing 21 let us go on their waiting list.

They told us that it could take a long time before they found something in either of the areas I'd specified we would like to live – near my mum, who lived in Salisbury, or near Allen's mum in Haslemere – but as it happened we were offered a house within two weeks.

I turned down the first one they showed us, but the next one was perfect: on a new estate in Clanfield, Hampshire, the village where I had been living when I first met Allen. Housing 21 would buy it and rent it back to us at an affordable rate. It was a small but pretty three-bedroom end-of-terrace house that was still being built, and after I saw it I said, 'Yes, please,' straight away. It would be good to be out of naval quarters and living somewhere that felt like our own. Also, I didn't want the Navy to be able to give me another shock like the one I'd had when those eviction papers dropped through the letterbox. I didn't think I'd survive another body blow like that.

In April 1993, we moved to our little house in Clanfield as a family. I had to arrange all the details of the move and find new schools for the children but I took that in my stride. There was no one else to do it; that's just the way it was.

And then, when we'd only been there a month, I had two family tragedies, one after the other. My father died suddenly of a massive heart attack at the age of sixty-five, and then my sister gave birth to a premature baby at thirty-two weeks. Little Alice, as she was called, lived for less than twenty-four hours. It was desperately sad, because my sister had lost other babies before, and the few hours Alice survived made us hope she was going to make it.

I asked Allen if he would come to Alice's funeral with me and he said no, he didn't want to. He gave no explanation. I didn't push him, but I felt very hurt and unsupported.

Shortly after that, we were at a case conference to talk about Allen and in the middle of it he complained to a case worker that it was 'all doom and gloom at home'.

I didn't say anything at the time but as soon as we got back to the house afterwards, I lost the plot. I really let him have it for the first time since he'd been injured. 'How can you be so bloody selfish?' I ranted. 'My dad's just died, my sister's baby's died, and you're complaining about doom and gloom?'

Then I shouted at him that when he was refusing to take the HIV test at Haslar, all he was worried about was his sexuality being questioned, when I was worried that he might have unknowingly infected our children and ruined their health for life. That hadn't even occurred to him. I was totally isolated, constantly battling his selfishness and making allowances for him, but when my children's health was affected, enough was enough.

And I yelled at him for being so selfish as to think he could just take an overdose and walk away from us all like that. 'What did you think you were doing? How dare you try to leave us? I know things are hard for you, but did you think for one minute about how you committing suicide would affect me and the kids? Did you? Don't you think you have some kind of responsibility towards us? Or is it just all about you you you?'

I was utterly at the end of my tether and I let rip with everything that was on my mind, then I threw my wedding ring at him and stormed out of the house, slamming the door behind me.

I drove to my friend Judy's house and sat with a cup of tea at her kitchen table, telling her all about it.

She listened, and when I'd finished she asked, 'Where is he now?'

'He's back at the house …' I replied. Then I started to panic. I shouldn't have left him alone when he was already psychologically fragile. What if he did something silly? I asked Judy to phone and see if he was still there, but there was no answer.

Seriously alarmed now, Judy and I drove back at full speed. We let ourselves into the house and searched it from top to bottom, including the garage, and every time I opened a door, my heart was pounding; I was terrified that Allen would be lying inside, collapsed on the floor. But he wasn't there. I noticed he had picked up my wedding ring and put it on the side. But where was he?

Not long after, the phone rang. It was HMS *Collingwood* saying that he had made his own way back and admitted himself to the sick bay. I asked if I could speak to him and when he came on the line, I said, 'Why did you leave?'

'Because I'm stuck with a woman I don't want to be with,' he replied. 'An angry woman whom I don't know and don't love.'

It was a complete slap on the face. I sank on to the sofa with my head in my hands, aware that I had reached rock bottom. This was the lowest point. I really hated the man my husband had become; all I wanted to do was walk away from the marriage. I'd worked and worked at getting our lives back on track and all I ever got from him in return was abuse. I'd been trying to convince myself that if I loved him enough and kept demonstrating that love, then eventually the man I married would come back, but now I was beginning to doubt that he ever would. It was as though I was trapped in a bad dream.

I went to bed that night wondering how it would work if I decided to take the children and leave Allen. Where would I go? What would we live on? What would happen to him? But when I woke up the next morning I knew I couldn't do it. I don't know what made me pick myself up and keep going. Maybe it was because of the love I'd had for the man he had once been. Maybe it was for the sake of the children. Maybe it was easier to continue on auto-pilot than to take any decisive action from which there would be no turning back.

I'd let everything get on top of me, and if I wasn't able to be strong for Allen, then we were both going to sink. Somehow I had to find the energy to pull both of us up again and find a way that we could carry on living – hopefully together.

CHAPTER THIRTEEN

Allen

I knew I was making some mistakes but I didn't think I was doing too badly at *Collingwood*. The moment of truth came on a day when there was a big war exercise on the base, something they do from time to time to check that everyone is familiar with the drills. There were fake bombs going off and thunder flashes everywhere and an officer ran up to me.

'Take this message to the main gate,' he ordered, and gave me a brief message to remember.

As he repeated it, I knew there was no way I was going to be able to remember it. It was physically impossible. However, I did remember the code you have to use during war exercises, and I said, 'Safeguard, no can do.'

'Safeguard' basically means something is 'real life' and not part of the exercise. If 'Fire! Fire!' is shouted during an exercise, then it's just part of the exercise. If 'Safeguard, fire!' is shouted, that means there really is a fire.

The officer looked at me, very shocked. 'Confirm, Chief Parton. No can do.' Then he moved on, but I knew I hadn't heard the last of it. That was a major wake-up call. You can't have dead weights in the Navy. They employ their fair share of disabled people, but everyone has to be able to do the job and react appropriately in an emergency. As the Navy gets smaller, it's more and more important that everyone, even those based on shore, is capable of going to sea if called upon. And the problem wasn't just that I was in a wheelchair and access to ships would be difficult; it was with my cognitive abilities. I didn't have the memory for the job any more. It was a defining moment, the point when I realized that my career in the Navy as I knew it was at an end.

As this knowledge sank in, I once again descended into the quicksand of my depression. If I couldn't work, I couldn't see the point of carrying on living. I'd been in loads of hospitals over the last two years and none of them had been able to cure me enough to make me capable of getting back to my job, or even a vaguely similar job. My feelings for Sandra and the children weren't strong enough to make me hesitate and take stock; I didn't feel I owed them anything. Anyway, they'd be better off without me. All I could see was a black pit of despair.

There was a mountaineering wall in one corner of the *Collingwood* gym, with handholds ascending up to the ceiling and ropes hanging down from the top. I sneaked in one day when there was no one else around and picked a rope that was dangling about three or four feet off the ground. I tied a slipknot in it, pushed myself up from my wheelchair with one hand and pulled the noose over my head. And then, with all my strength, I threw myself out of the chair, shoving it away.

My useless legs crumpled under me and the noose jerked tight around my throat, choking me. There was a creaking sound and I felt myself falling to the floor, then I landed with a thump and the metal handhold clattered down just beside my head. It had only been spot-welded in place and couldn't take the jolt caused by my weight suddenly pulling, so had been wrenched out of its sockets.

It was a massive handhold, the type you would normally find welded to the side of a ship. I imagine they got them from the dockyard. I lay on the floor looking at this big metal object weighing several kilos and I realized that if it had fallen just a couple of inches to the right, it would have landed on my head and would certainly have killed me. For a moment I felt annoyed that their shoddy workmanship could have finished me off, before I realized the irony.

Seconds later, people came rushing in to the gym. Those who found me can have had no doubt about my intentions because of the rope around my neck. I was rushed to the sick bay and people were crowding round, and some of them must have known what had happened but others just seemed to think I'd fallen out of my wheelchair. It was all very unclear and I don't remember it very well.

I was checked over and sent home but after that I wasn't allowed to go to the gym any more. I think my Navy bosses realized that I was too unstable to continue being employed by them. I was a liability rather than an asset. In November 1993 I received some official papers asking me to attend a medical board at Haslar naval hospital on the 30th of the month at 11 a.m.

I was very nervous when I turned up to face the board. Sandra came with me but she was asked to wait outside. There were five men sitting around the table and it didn't take long at all. I thought I'd be questioned and allowed to put across my own point of view, but in fact I realize now that they had made up their minds before I entered the room. The board was just a formality to tell me that I was being medically discharged and my contract with the Navy terminated after eighteen years.

Despite everything that had happened, I swear I was shocked and extremely surprised. I suppose I was expecting them to find something else for me to do, maybe an office job that wasn't on an active base. Instead, things happened very quickly. Once the decision was made they wanted me out straight away. Sandra and I were given the papers to apply for a war pension and shown the door, so to speak.

'Do I have time to go back and get …?'

'No, you're out!'

'Can I say goodbye to …?'

'No.'

And then suddenly you're a civilian and there's no infrastructure to help you. You just hand in your uniform and your gas mask and service equipment and that's it. There's no school to teach you how to be a civilian, no careers advice, no further medical help. I lost my job, my future and my hope all in one go.

CHAPTER FOURTEEN

Sandra

I was prepared for the worst the day we went to the medical board. Allen seemed very dazed when we came out, but I don't think he expressed any emotion to me. I felt desperately sorry for him but we didn't really discuss it. I had to get busy straight away sorting out all the business of going back to civilian life. We had to hand back our ID badges and military cards, and I was given the forms to apply for a war pension.

That was a laborious process. I had to compile medical reports and service reports and all sorts of pieces of paperwork. I sent it all off and waited a few weeks. When word came back that our request was being refused on the grounds that what Allen was doing at the time he was injured – going for dinner with ex-pats – wasn't considered 'active duty', I burst into tears. They tried to make out that it was his time off and that he was at leisure when it happened. How were we expected to live? Were we meant to slip away quietly and sign on the dole?

I suppose I was becoming quite good at battling authority, one way or another. It's not in my basic nature but when you have to do something to protect your family you just find the strength from somewhere. I was upset but I was also enraged and once again I sought legal advice. I found out that war pensions are notoriously difficult to procure. It's not an automatic right. It took us months and months and dozens of letters backwards and forwards before they finally accepted that when service personnel are away from home on a tour of duty, they are officially considered to be on active duty twenty-four hours a day, so Allen could get his pension after all. He'd have to have annual medical checks to confirm his condition still prevented him from working, but that was fine. It was a huge relief when it was all sorted out.

Since May 1993 I'd been working as a volunteer at an organization called the Help and Information Volunteer Exchange, or HIVE, a drop-in centre for naval families where they could get advice on any problems they were having. It was useful learning about how all the internal navy systems worked and what the regulations were, but after Allen was discharged I was told I couldn't work there any more because the counsellors were supposed to be naval wives. I thought it was a shame because after all the bureaucracy I'd battled with over the years since Allen was injured,

I had very good experience of the services and could have given great advice to anyone who needed to know their rights and how to make the system work for them.

We received a lump sum payment from the Navy, known as gratuities, based on the number of years of Allen's service, and I decided to spend some of this on a family holiday. I plumped for Disney World in Orlando, Florida, because Allen and I had taken the kids there when they were aged three and two and everything had worked very smoothly. I knew the resort was well set up for children and the disabled, so I figured I'd be able to cope.

Everything on the trip went reasonably well. Zoe had her birthday out there and we had a 'character breakfast' with all the Disney characters serenading her. Allen rolled around in a big old hospital wheelchair but he made a mistake a more experienced wheelchair-user would never have done by wearing shorts without sunscreen and got his knees badly sunburned. Of course, when you're in a wheelchair, your knees are directly exposed to the rays. Liam had a good time except that he managed to dent the door of our hire car by backing into it with his bottom; fortunately I managed to pull it out again using a loo plunger I borrowed from the hotel so we didn't get charged.

Once we were back home, however, the holiday mood quickly evaporated and Allen was back to his usual grumpy, taciturn self. I needed to find something for him to do during the day, because he would have driven me to distraction if he'd been under my feet the whole time. Thankfully,

I found out about a day-care centre in Portsmouth called the Horizon Centre, where he could be looked after from nine in the morning through to five in the afternoon. It was run by Hampshire Health Authority so wouldn't cost us anything. We applied for this and he was approved to start attending in August 1994. He didn't go every single day – we also had what I called our Darby and Joan days when I dragged him round to help with whatever I was doing. We went to the supermarket, the garden centre, clothes shopping, or visiting my mum, his mum or his granddad – just normal everyday stuff. He was very antisocial, though, and not very communicative if well-meaning folk tried to engage him in conversation. They'd be more likely to get snapped at than greeted.

Allen wasn't good at putting names to faces. If we bumped into our next-door neighbours in the high street, chances are he wouldn't recognize them and would blurt out: 'Who are you?' I was always telling him that sounded rude but he couldn't see it. Our neighbours got used to it after a while and would even make a joke out of it, introducing themselves mock-formally every time we met.

At home he was still struggling to manage without a wheelchair, just dragging himself round by the arms, hanging on to furniture and walls and the like to support his weight, while his legs trailed uselessly behind. This was all very well and I could understand it, but it was painfully slow if he tried to manage without a chair when we went to the shops. He could get himself out of the car and haul himself round it by holding on to the roof rack but he would then be stuck if there was nothing else to hang on to.

'You'll tire yourself out that way,' I cajoled. 'Why not use a wheelchair when we go out somewhere and you can get yourself around when you're back at home?'

'I am *not* disabled!' he yelled at me.

'I know you're not,' I said. 'It's just for now, just for today.'

Eventually he agreed – he knew he couldn't go out without one any more – but he sulked about it whenever he was in a chair.

We had absolutely no social life in those days. We didn't go out to the cinema or to restaurants, although I suppose we could have done if we'd wanted to. It just seemed too complicated to get a babysitter and go to a restaurant where they would seat you at the back beside the toilet so the wheelchair didn't get in anyone's way.

Allen's social difficulties meant I was reluctant to have people round to the house because he might upset them by being abrupt, or brutally honest. He wouldn't hesitate to say something like, 'That colour makes you look really fat,' for example, and few people could cope with him. His speech still wasn't very clear so, fortunately, quite often when he was being blunt people couldn't make his words out, but it could be extremely awkward.

He couldn't follow a normal conversation very well, so we might be chatting about politics, say, and Allen would burst in with a comment on the weather. We never even had conversations with each other beyond simple domestic things like 'What do you fancy for dinner tonight?' I became a hermit, seeing my own friends for coffee while Allen was at the day centre and staying in at weekends and in the evenings.

It was a basic, sterile existence, two strangers rubbing along side by side and occasionally erupting into furious argument. He still looked at me sometimes with an expression of pure irritation that bordered on hatred and I felt like bursting into tears. What had I ever done to deserve this? What more could I do for him?

Allen's sister Suzanne took him out a couple of times to take the pressure off me, but they fell out and so that stopped. His mum wasn't strong enough to cope with him on her own so it was hard for me to get a break. All the responsibility for looking after my husband and children lay at my feet and I just had to get on with it.

When Zoe was seven, I'd had a wake-up call that I needed to focus on the children more. My arrangement that a neighbour would pick her up from school fell through and she was left standing in the playground for two hours before I realized what had happened. The teachers had tried to phone but hadn't been able to track me down, because of course those were the days before we all had mobiles. When I got there she was in floods of tears, her little face bright red, and I felt dreadful that she had been so badly let down. I hugged her tight but she couldn't stop shaking with fear and sobs.

I think she lost faith in grown-ups after that. Her daddy had gone away, and when he came back he was different than he had been before; her granddad (my father) went away and didn't come back; and my sister's baby Alice went away as well; and so she started to worry about being left anywhere in case no one came back to get her. She refused to go to Brownies any more unless I stayed in the hall throughout and she became very reluctant to go to school. It took a lot of coaxing and one-to-one chats to try and help her to feel secure again.

Allen didn't help because once he was back at home living with us full-time he started to clash with Zoe. She's noisier than Liam and more likely to stick up for herself and she used to pester him sometimes, just looking for attention. One evening I heard them arguing in the kitchen.

'Will you stop that bloody racket?' he shouted.

I couldn't hear her reply, but seconds later there was an ominous thudding sound. I hurried into the kitchen and saw that Allen had pinned her to the wall.

'Stop it! Leave her alone!' I screamed, grabbing his arm.

His grip loosened and Zoe wriggled away and ran out of the room crying. He swivelled the chair round so his back was to me.

'Allen, she's only little. You can't do that to her.'

He didn't reply, just started bashing pots around in the sink to drown out my voice.

I don't like to think what might have happened if I hadn't intervened. He frequently lost his temper when she was winding him up, and didn't seem to make allowance for the fact that she was only a kid. Anyone else would just have said, 'Oh, for goodness' sake, clear off!' but Allen exploded and scared us all.

Zoe just wanted her dad back the way he used to be and she'd push and push for him to do the things he used to do, unable to comprehend that he wasn't capable any more. She'd climb on to his lap on the wheelchair but he would pinch her legs to make her get off again. Sometimes he pinched too hard and gave her nasty bruises, just because he didn't know his own strength any more.

Around this period, I must admit I consulted a solicitor to find out what the position would be if I left Allen. Would I be entitled to maintenance payments for the children from his war pension? Where could we live? I got the information and tucked it away in the back of my mind in case things got any worse. I didn't want to split my family up; I would much rather bring them closer together if I could, but I was running out of ideas.

That autumn I watched a documentary presented by Jill Dando about the facilities for the disabled at a ski resort called Winter Park in Denver, Colorado, and it looked wonderful. The mountains were stunning, the accommodation was modern and comfortable and there was loads to do out there when you weren't skiing.

Allen had loved skiing in the old days and been quite a champion. According to this programme they had special 'sit skis' for the disabled – basically a chair on skis. I called Allen to come and have a look and he seemed enthusiastic. The kids hadn't tried skiing before but there were classes for all age groups and they were keen to have a go.

I was apprehensive about the idea of taking them all away somewhere we'd never been but I'd always loved family holidays in the past. I thought they were very bonding and it would be good to think we could manage it again.

Before we got there, there was the journey to contemplate. Florida had been a direct flight but this time we had to change in New York. It was a hassle getting Allen to the airport, along with kids and luggage, and then on and off the plane. On arrival in New York we had to wait till everyone else got off, then they raised the little hydraulic platform that brought fresh supplies of food and drink for the next flight so he could be lowered to ground level in his wheelchair.

We got through to immigration where there were huge long queues at every desk and my heart sank. This was going to take hours and I had two jet-lagged children to control. Then a uniformed man came up to us.

'Hi there, can I help you guys? Come this way, please.'

I thought: Oh God, we're going to be searched for contraband, but instead he pushed us right to the front of the queue and through some barriers, then they closed the gate behind us and asked for our passports.

When they looked at Allen's passport, they could see right away he'd been in the military. He had stamps on his passport from Iran, Iraq and other war-torn places around the world.

'Were you in action in the Gulf, sir?' they asked.

I explained that he'd been injured in the Gulf War.

'It wasn't blue on blue, was it?'

I didn't know what that meant, so I turned to Allen and he shook his head. He explained later that it meant 'friendly fire'. Unfortunately it was a common phenomenon in that first Gulf War.

'Thank you very much, sir,' the immigration officer said, handing the passports back to Allen, then he shook his hand. We were ushered out with the utmost respect, having jumped to the front of the never-ending queue, and I was astonished to find that we'd been upgraded to first class for the second leg of our journey. It was only our first taste of the amazing care that Americans take of the disabled and their huge respect for war veterans.

Once we got to the resort, I was relieved to find that the programme had been accurate and it really was well set up for someone in a wheelchair. The rooms were accessible, they had ramps as an alternative wherever there were flights of stairs, and the instructors who helped Allen into his sit ski were fantastic. I took some wonderful photos of him grinning from ear to ear as he swept down the slopes, reaching speeds as fast as the non-disabled skiers, which was important to him because he's always been competitive. His personality changed with the accident and many of his former qualities were lost but the competitiveness remains full on.

An instructor said to Allen, 'You have no fear, do you?'

And he quipped, 'What's the worst that could happen? That I could end up in a wheelchair?'

I think he broke the springs on a couple of their sit skis as he whizzed over moguls and zigzagged through the woods but they didn't complain and I was just glad to see him having such a good time.

The kids enjoyed their first taste of skiing – although Liam also got addicted to watching *Power Rangers* back on the hotel's big TV. It was an all-round success and definitely put Allen in a better frame of mind.

But, as before, it evaporated as soon as we got back to our tiny, cramped home again and he had to cope with the realities of life in a wheelchair, with his range of physiological problems and no career to keep him occupied. We couldn't have holidays the whole time. Somehow I had to come up with something else to make my family unit work.

CHAPTER FIFTEEN

Allen

Sandra panicked when she was faced with the prospect of having me at home twenty-four hours a day, seven days a week. She's a strong woman but she knew how bad-tempered and demanding I could be, and she just couldn't face the thought of having me to look after as well as the kids.

Someone recommended a day-care centre in Portsmouth, called the Horizon Centre, and that seemed just the thing. I'd be picked up in a minibus at nine o'clock in the morning every weekday, driven to the centre, then collected and brought home again about six, so that gave Sandra time to deal with the kids' homework, get the tea on and have a bit of a life of her own as well. I went along with it, but it was hard at first. The journey took an hour and a half each way because we had to stop and pick up half a dozen other people and the process of getting them on and off the bus was tedious as some were painfully slow. As we drove over the hill on the outskirts of Portsmouth, I could see all the way down to the dockyard and the sea and that was like rubbing salt in the wounds. It was painful to accept that my naval career really was over, and that I was now an outsider.

One of my main emotions was guilt: guilt that I wasn't still out there with the other lads serving my country but had skulked home injured, no use to anyone any more. It felt as though I was on the scrap heap at the age of thirty-four.

I still felt furious that all my problems had come about through no fault of my own. It simply wasn't fair, and it made me angry with the universe. I took it out on everyone around me and especially Sandra. She was the one who was there day to day and that's why she got the brunt of it. Who else could I kick out at? There were days when nothing she did was right and I'm sure she breathed a sigh of relief when the day-care bus picked me up in the morning.

Although there were a few naval people at the Horizon Centre, it was mainly men who were coming up to pensionable age, at which point they would be transferred over to the old people's day-care centre. The activities were very unchallenging: we'd sit and listen to classical music, which was known as 'music therapy'. We'd plan a dinner menu, go off to the supermarket and buy the ingredients, then come back to the centre and cook it: simple things like beef stew or spaghetti bolognese. Sometimes we did baking and I became a dab hand at making rock cakes, which the kids scoffed when I took them home. We went out on untaxing day trips to stately homes or gardens or museums. That first Christmas, we had a party at which I got howling drunk and Sandra was very unimpressed when I came rolling home off the minibus.

It was very depressing at the centre. I felt we were being treated like children, and I hated being lumped in with the elderly as though I had no further purpose in life. From fine-tuning missile systems I was reduced to stirring cake mix.

One useful thing that happened at the centre was that I got to practise using home computers. We'd had some big complicated computers in the Navy back in 1991, before I was injured, but I'd never run Windows or surfed the Internet before. I was immediately interested and started spending as much time as I could teaching myself all the functions. I couldn't remember how to spell and my words came out all scrambled, but someone introduced me to a fantastic programme designed for dyslexics that made sense of the words I did type, and a whole new method of communication was opened to me at a time when I still couldn't speak very fluently.

I persuaded Sandra that we should get a computer at home.

Our first one was an AST computer that we got on hire purchase from Radio Rentals. It was very basic but I enjoyed learning how to play games on it – Patience was a favourite. It was just something to keep my mind ticking over. I knew I still had the basic intelligence that had enabled me to design weapons systems. When I tried to work something out on the computer, I could use logic to reach conclusions and I became pretty good quite fast, if I say so myself. My memory remained the problem, though, and that was just incredibly frustrating.

I still felt alienated from Sandra and the children once I was back at home full-time. We were strangers forced to live under the same roof. I really hated being dependent on them if I dropped something and couldn't reach it, for example if it rolled under the table. I could get myself to the loo and make myself a snack and I could get from my chair into bed, or into the car, but everything was slow and laborious and draining. My wheelchair was cumbersome and the furniture in our tiny house was so tightly packed that if one of the kids moved something it made it impossible for me to squeeze through and get to the kitchen or the toilet, which was infuriating.

That big old red hospital wheelchair was so difficult to manoeuvre that as soon as we got back from our holiday in Orlando Sandra suggested I should use some of the gratuities money to buy a custom-made chair. I didn't need much persuading. Using a hospital wheelchair is like wearing someone else's pants; it didn't fit my bottom. I did some research and bought a stunning white chair with a jazzy splash of colour on the wheels, all measured and fitted exactly, and it was incredibly comfortable. I suppose that was an important moment. I suppose that was me beginning to accept I was wheelchair-bound and likely to remain that way for the foreseeable future.

There was no room for a stairlift. If I needed a sweater from the bedroom upstairs during the daytime, I had to sit on my bottom and pull myself up step by step, and then at the top I could sit on the edge of the table on which Zoe's dolls' house was kept and shuffle along to our room. It was exhausting, but I preferred to do that rather than ask someone to fetch the sweater for me.

My short-term memory was appalling. I could get to the end of a sentence now without forgetting the beginning but I couldn't remember what I'd done the day before, so if I woke up in the morning and Sandra seemed to be in the huff with me I'd have no idea why.

'I thought you would be saying sorry to me,' she'd snap indignantly.

I'd stare at her in confusion because I had no idea what I'd done. Was it better to ask and risk a rehash of the whole argument, whatever it had been about, or just ignore it and hope it would blow over? How I reacted depended on how I was feeling that day.

We slept together in a big double bed, but it was a very sterile relationship. There was no cuddling, nothing like that. We just put the lights out and fell asleep. To me she was my nurse and my carer, and sometimes she could be a bit of a nag. I know I irritated the hell out of her with my short-temperedness and stroppiness but I was burning up with frustration and she was the only person I had to take it out on.

I used to sit in my own little insular world, not even trying to communicate with anyone else. I was angry and bitter and resentful and rebuffed any attempts to reach out to me. Looking back, I've got no idea why she put up with it. She could easily have walked out and I would probably have ended up in some kind of war pensioners' home – but she didn't because Sandra's not a quitter. I'm sure there were times when she went to bed thinking: That's it. I'll leave him in the morning, but then she would just wake up and plod on.

My old Navy friend Kevin knew that Sandra needed a break but it was hard to think what I was capable of. A couple of years later, in 1997, he offered to take me to a sporting event in the States organized by the Paralyzed Veterans of America. The British Legion were sending out a team to the National Veterans' Wheelchair Games in San Diego and they invited me to go as a guest, so Kevin kindly agreed to come along to look after me.

I don't think I was great company for him. My speech still wasn't very good, but I was able to be argumentative and I remember we argued in a pub one night where I thought they were refusing to serve me. I was being so stubborn that he threatened to walk off and leave me. But fundamentally Kevin was a good mate, who's bent over backwards to help out since my injury. He dug the garden, bought presents for the kids, fixed the electrics if Sandra needed it, and now he was giving her a break by taking me on holiday – although I still hated the fact that I needed someone to 'babysit' me.

I remember several of the events from the games. There was an archery contest for people in wheelchairs, and their dogs were trained to go and fetch their arrows for them, which was useful. And I saw one guy sending his dog over to get him a drink, which impressed me. In retrospect, I probably spent more time watching the dogs than the athletes.

The spirit of the games was amazing. I remember one guy in a wheelchair who had very little movement at all in his upper body asked if he could be entered in the 100 metres race. It took him forty-five minutes to complete the course, and the whole stadium clapped and cheered him right along the track to the finishing line. If anyone had gone to help push him he'd have been disqualified, so they just left him to finish by himself and a huge roar went up. It was very moving.

Kevin and I talked a bit about my disabilities and he was good at teasing out my worries and getting me to talk. I tried to explain to him that I still saw life as black or white, good or bad, and basically the life I was capable of since my accident wasn't good. It wasn't good at all.

He tried to point out all the things I could do from a chair and mentioned the fulfilling lives that the athletes we'd been watching had, but I wasn't ready to listen. I was definitely in a glass-half-empty – or a glass-totally-empty – frame of mind.

We had some big all-you-can-eat American dinners, and drank beer and sat up late, and I suppose the holiday did cheer me up a bit, but then I came back to our tiny house in Clanfield and the struggle of my day-to-day life in close proximity to a wife and children I didn't feel any connection with and I was right back at rock bottom again.

My disabilities were like a cancer at the heart of the family, eating away at us all. I found out from the British Legion that out of ninety-eight married servicemen who were seriously injured in the First Gulf War, only five of their marriages survived. They had a range of injuries – loss of legs, burns, broken backs and so forth – but it was the emotional aspect of the return to civilian life as a disabled person that destroyed their families.

Our children were brought up by their mother. I never looked after them, got them drinks of juice, helped with homework, played with them or took any responsibility whatsoever for their care. My excuse was that it took me all my time to look after myself, but it meant that the family unit as a whole wasn't working. We only kept going because Sandra looked after all the practicalities and bent over backwards to keep us together.

No one in the world would have blamed Sandra if she had left me. Kevin had pointed that out to me and I knew he was right. But instead of walking away she battled on, taking care of us all, year after year. Looking back, I don't know how she did it. In her position, I know I couldn't have put up with the sheer drudgery of her life, and the loneliness of not having anyone to share things with.

CHAPTER SIXTEEN

Sandra

Part of the problem I faced in trying to improve our home life was that the house we were living in was far too small for two lanky kids, who were growing up fast, and a man in a cumbersome wheelchair. I approached the charity Housing 21 and asked if there was any chance we could be moved to a bigger house. I had seen some new houses being built locally that had adjoining garages, and I had the idea that I could convert the garage into a room for Allen where he could get away from the kids and do his own thing. I also planned to add a conservatory at the back where I could get some peace myself away from blaring TVs and stereos and squabbling children.

I found a house I liked that hadn't been sold and sent the details to Housing 21 to see if they would buy it then rent it back to us, as they did with the house we were in. They considered it for a while but then pulled out and I was upset and frustrated because I'd set my heart on it by this time.

I tried to get a mortgage, but the first question building societies asked was: 'Are you or your husband employed?' and they slammed the door in my face when the answer was 'No'. Allen's war pension was for life and would continue to be paid to me after his death so it was a guaranteed income, but no one wanted to give us a mortgage based on it. He couldn't get life insurance either and I didn't like to think about the implications of that.

Then two things happened that rescued us. Allen's friend Kevin offered to lend us a deposit, and the builders of the house, who hadn't found any other buyers, said they would reduce the price and help us to get a mortgage deal. It all fell into place and we packed up and moved to our lovely new house, just round the corner from the old one, in April 1995. It was the first home we had actually owned ourselves and I was over the moon. It makes all the difference when you own rather than rent and I enjoyed choosing curtains and fittings and getting it all the way I wanted it.

Moving made me think back to all the plans we had had before the accident, for the dream home that we were going to buy. The picture I'd had in my head was an idealized one of a detached house with a big garden, with a swing for the kids and lots of flowers. The place we'd just bought wasn't like that – the garden was quite small and it was semi-detached – but it was in an area we both liked and I was very pleased with it.

A year after we arrived in the new house, it was time to start thinking about choosing a secondary school for Liam, who was eleven years old. I went to visit the local comprehensive, which had 2,500 pupils, and I didn't think it would be good for him. Since his father's accident, Liam had become quite introverted. He never talked about what had happened but he had lost his male role model and his best Lego mate and that's hard for a young boy. He didn't cry and have tantrums but he never talked about what he was feeling either. I think he became very private because he felt he couldn't express himself freely in the house with Allen around, so he just decided to keep his thoughts to himself.

Unlike other kids their age, mine couldn't invite their friends over to play and I think Liam became a bit of a loner. When I met any of his peers, I realized his social skills weren't as well developed as theirs. He certainly wasn't one of the 'in' crowd.

Anyway, I did my research and decided that I wanted him to go to an independent school in Petersfield, which would be small enough for him to get individual attention from his teachers, and where the crowds in the playground wouldn't be so overwhelming. They had government-assisted places on offer, but when I phoned up I was told they had all been allocated.

'Can we come and see you anyway?' I asked, just to get a foot in the door.

Allen, Liam and I went for a family interview with the headmaster, but Liam hardly said a word, and when he was asked for a private one-to-one chat with the headmaster he flatly refused to go in on his own. First he tried to run out of the door, and then he crumpled in a heap and burst into tears. I think he found the atmosphere very intimidating.

The headmaster said, 'I don't want to be cruel, but I'm afraid this is not the kind of school for someone who can't cope with pressure.'

I said, 'Yes, I quite understand. But I wonder if I could have five minutes of your time to explain our situation?' Allen and Liam were shown out and once the door closed behind them, I gave the speech of my life. I had no choice; my son's future was at stake and the responsibility for sorting it out was all mine.

I told him about Allen's accident and what it was like for the children growing up for the last few years without a proper, hands-on father, although they had someone who looked the same as their old dad sitting in a wheelchair in the corner. I explained that if Liam was a bit immature it was because he had had a very disrupted childhood to date. I said that he was bright but he needed personal encouragement and I was scared that he would disappear into the system as just another number if he went to the local comprehensive. I talked and I talked and finally, when I had finished, the headmaster said that Liam could come and do a trial day at the school to see how he got on.

Fortunately the trial day must have gone well because in the end the headmaster not only agreed that Liam could come to his school, but he also said that he would find an extra government-assisted place for him.

I was very proud of myself and delighted by the outcome, but I couldn't help reflecting that this wasn't the life I had thought I was going to have back when we got married twelve and a half years earlier. When we'd planned our future, we'd agreed that once the children went to secondary school I would stop following Allen from base to base and establish a secure home for us all in one spot. Now we were setting up a home in one place but for quite different, much sadder reasons.

I'd assumed that I would work part-time once the kids were at school, but I thought my earnings would pay for extras like holidays and that Allen would always be the main wage-earner. We'd hoped that Allen would have a couple more promotions before he retired and we'd have had a lot more money to play with. Once we found out the extent of his war pension, however, we realized that money was going to be tight. We'd be hard-pressed to support two teenagers and see them through college to whatever careers they decided they wanted to pursue, but how could I take a job when I had Allen to look after? We'd just have to scrape by somehow.

I tried not to look backwards, but if only we had been able to claim a lump sum compensation for Allen's accident, we would have been able to buy a nice house outright and fit it with disabled ramps and lifts and so forth. Still, at least we had a roof over our heads, even if we couldn't afford to do the garage conversion and build the conservatory I wanted straight away.

A year after Liam started secondary school, it was Zoe's turn. She is quite a different personality from Liam – a complete chatterbox, very trusting and outgoing. In fact, she's just like Allen used to be before his accident. Her confidence was dented by Allen's problems, though, and they continued to argue a lot at home.

When it was time for Zoe to go to secondary school, a charity called the Royal Naval and Royal Marines Children's Trust came up trumps and paid for her to go to an excellent girls' school, the Royal School in Haslemere. The Queen is its patron and it has historic naval connections. About a third of the girls there are boarders and Zoe liked it so much that after a couple of years, when she was fourteen, she asked us if she could become a weekly boarder. I didn't want her to. I'd always felt that boarding school forces children to grow up too quickly when they should still be allowed to be children and I knew I would miss her terribly. But our house was so cramped that her being away from Monday to Friday helped to relieve some of the pressure at home and at least it stopped her clashing with Allen.

We struggled along as best as we could in the meantime. I was very grateful when Allen's old friend Kevin, who had been best man at our wedding and had been incredibly supportive since the accident, kindly agreed to take Allen to San Diego to watch the Paralyzed Veterans of America Annual Games in 1997. He'd been invited by the British Legion but couldn't go on his own. I think it was inspiring for him to see all these disabled people who refused to let their physical handicaps limit them. That's certainly what Kevin had in mind. I was very grateful and thought what a great friend he was for doing that.

When he got back from San Diego, I remember Allen talking about the assistance dogs some disabled athletes used. He was impressed with their intelligence and dedication to their owners and the way he went on about it may have planted a little seed in my brain. Allen had always liked dogs and so had I. I didn't know much about assistance dogs at the time but it started me thinking. I had to come up with some way of changing our lives. I didn't know what it would be but I knew I couldn't go on as we were long-term and I was so desperate I was prepared to clutch at any straws. We were two unhappy, lonely people existing together in the same house and just managing by the skin of our teeth. The marriage was like a leaking boat. If I stopped bailing out water for even a minute, we were going to sink.

Back in January 1997, before Allen's trip to San Diego, there had been an article in our local paper about an organization called Canine Partners for Independence, which trained assistance dogs for people with disabilities. I'd heard of guide dogs for the blind before, but I didn't know much about dogs for people with disabilities. I read that they could work with all kinds of disability, and the dog owners included people with MS, cerebral palsy, spinal injuries, arthritis and all kinds of other debilitating illnesses. Some had limited mobility while others were completely dependent on carers. I was amazed to read that by the end of their training the dogs could respond to at least thirty different commands, and they were carefully matched and taught specific skills to suit the needs of the disabled person they would be working with.

The article said that they were desperate for volunteer puppy walkers to take on puppies for the first fourteen months of their lives and do their basic care and training, before they went on an intensive training programme and were assigned to the disabled person they would be working for. I clipped the piece out of the newspaper and put it to one side.

Six months later, I happened to see a woman in a wheelchair accompanied by an assistance dog and it jogged my memory. The dog seemed very intelligent and they made a great team. I remembered Allen talking about the dogs at the games in San Diego and it struck a chord for me. I came home, dug out the article and phoned the number at the bottom.

'I wanted to find out about becoming a puppy walker,' I said.

The woman replied, 'There's a puppy class going on at the moment. Why don't you pop down and watch so you can see what's involved?'

She gave me the address and I drove straight there. It was a big old shed rather than slick, professional-looking offices. There were six puppies that day – Labradors, golden retrievers, poodles, and dogs that looked like mixtures of these – along with their puppy walkers and a couple of instructors. They were playing a game of musical mats – the doggy equivalent of musical chairs. When the music was playing they had to run around, but once it stopped their puppy walker had to get them to lie down on a mat as fast as they could. One of the trainers explained to me that it was part of the process of getting them to respond instantly to commands rather than sitting around thinking about them.

The puppy walkers were all different types of people, aged from their twenties through to their sixties. On that day it was all women, and when I spoke to them I found that some were young mothers who had a bit of spare time on their hands after the kids started school, while others were recently retired, and they came from a variety of backgrounds.

One woman stood out because she had a distinctive, very well-spoken voice. She was calling: 'Endal! Endal! Endal!' in an excitable tone and I remember thinking to myself what a stupid name that was for a dog.

I noticed that all the older dogs had names beginning with 'E' – Echo, Errol, Endal – while the younger ones had names beginning with 'F' – Ferdy, Flame, Flynn. Someone explained to me that every six months they start a new team, and the incoming puppies are given names beginning with the next letter of the alphabet.

They were all wearing a red Canine Partners 'puppy in training' jacket. I learned that once they graduated and got an assistance dog jacket this gave them legal rights of access to shops and so forth under the Disability Act. When a dog is wearing the jacket, they can't be refused entry anywhere their owner goes.

After the class was over, I had a chat with the puppy trainer, Tessa. I explained about our home situation and she said that it was ideal that we were there during the day and that we had children, because it was good for the puppies to get accustomed to kids. She said the fact that Allen was in a wheelchair could also be good because the puppy would get used to being around disability, although that wasn't something they would look for in every family.

She explained that you kept puppies for fourteen months and during that time you had to attend weekly training classes. It was very important that you stuck to all the techniques you learned and were strict about the puppy's training at home, because that could make all the difference to whether it would be able to work as an assistance dog one day. She said it was a big responsibility and they'd have to come and check the house to make sure our facilities were adequate.

I said that would be fine.

She also explained that you get very attached to the puppies but have to prepare yourself for the fact that they'll be taken away from you at fourteen months old, if not before. They arranged frequent 'puppy swaps' to help the dogs get socialized, so they might have a couple of weeks with an elderly person, or in a home with cats or other dogs. It was good for them to get used to the changes from an early age.

'Do you think you could cope with that?' she asked.

'Definitely,' I replied emphatically. 'How long would it be before we could have a puppy?'

She glanced down at some notes on her desk. 'It could be two or three months. We'll let you know.'

'I thought you were desperate for puppy walkers? That's what it said in the article.'

'That's right. We're keen to have plenty on our books because we want to expand and train more dogs in the next few years.'

I went home feeling disappointed things weren't going to happen faster, because the more I heard about puppy walking the keener I was to do it. It was such a worthwhile cause, the dogs were so cute, and I knew I would enjoy the challenge. My life was very busy already, but I needed something that was more fulfilling than domestic drudgery.

Ten days later I got a phone call from Tessa at Canine Partners. 'Is there any chance we can come to your house to vet you today? It's just that there's a puppy we need to rehome as soon as possible and I think it might be a suitable one for you.'

They came and had a look round the house and met Allen and agreed that everything was fine, and the next day an eight-week-old yellow Labrador called Ferdy was delivered to us. He was a lively fellow, and the children adored him. This was the first dog they'd ever had and they would sit on the floor playing with him for hours on end, teasing him with a bit of rope and wrestling toys from his mouth.

Ferdy was a funny character, who used to carry his own pillow around with him, and when he was tired he would lie down and have a sleep on it. Zoe made him a cushion of his own and embroidered his name on it. I'd been worried about how the rabbits we kept in the garden would cope with the new arrival but they seemed to accept each other's presence without question.

It was my responsibility to do all the obedience training and go to the weekly puppy classes. First of all, Ferdy had to learn to use a special toilet area I created in the back garden. Then he had to become accustomed to spending time lying quietly in his crate, without chewing or barking or running wild. This was important because he might have to lie quietly for long periods when accompanying the disabled person he was assigned to, perhaps at hospital appointments or meetings. All the Canine Partners puppies spent several hours a day resting in their crates as part of the training, and that provides a welcome relief for the puppy parents, because when they're out of the crates you need to keep a close eye on them to see they don't get up to mischief, such as stealing food, or into danger, perhaps by chewing electric cables.

What a puppy learns in the first sixteen weeks is crucial. Assistance dogs need to learn good basic manners, such as not barging ahead of you through doors, not barking inappropriately, sitting when asked, coming when called, and walking nicely on a loose lead. They can't be allowed to tear up your kitchen lino or run amok in public. It's crucial that they don't get overexcited and rush off suddenly in a way that could pull a disabled person from their wheelchair. You have to be very strict with them, as with a toddler, and my role was to do the obedience training.

As a first-time puppy walker learning the ropes, I made some mistakes with Ferdy and maybe wasn't as strict as I should have been. Unless you are 100 per cent consistent with the rules, the dogs get confused and don't know what they are supposed to be doing, but Ferdy turned out just fine. He was a very nice dog, eager to do the right thing.

Allen seemed pleased to have a dog in the house. He liked to sit with Ferdy on his lap where he could pet him, but he made it clear he didn't want to get involved in any of the training. Since he got back from his trip to the US with Kevin, he'd been feeling particularly sorry for himself. Maybe having had a taste of freedom from the prison of our domestic situation made it feel even more oppressive to come back to.

He still didn't accept that he was going to be disabled for the rest of his life, but he slipped into the role of the invalid, letting other people do things for him and not taking any responsibility. We often argued because I felt that he should be doing as much as he could for himself – peeling potatoes, doing the washing-up, hanging out laundry, and so forth – whereas he was happy to be waited on hand and foot. If I didn't nag him, he wouldn't do anything at all, and that wasn't like the man I had married. I was getting sick and tired of being his carer instead of his partner and not being able to see any likelihood of things getting better. It seemed to me that the only way our marriage was going to survive was if he became as independent of me as he possibly could and it dismayed me that he was happy for me to be the carer.

However, I found a new focus for myself once I started training Ferdy. I looked forward to my weekly puppy class and spent a lot of time working with him, trying to make sure he knew all the techniques well in advance so that he would shine in front of the trainers. I was so keen that it wasn't long before Tessa asked if I would like to become a puppy class helper – which meant assisting other puppy walkers at the weekly classes, and setting out the equipment we needed. Needless to say, I was delighted to do this.

You work hard with a young puppy to establish the relationship but there is a real sense of achievement when they begin to respond. They give back a lot of affection, which makes it all the more rewarding. It reminded me of many of the aspects of nursing that I used to enjoy: caring for others and knowing that you are helping them. With Allen I slaved away caring for him but never got any appreciation or sense that I was achieving anything.

Then Canine Partners asked if I would be prepared to give talks at various local events to help them to recruit more puppy walkers. I was a bit unsure about this, because I'm quite shy by nature and hadn't done any public speaking before.

'It's easy,' Tessa said. 'You don't need a long, prepared speech. All you need to do is chat about what it's like being a puppy walker. You seem so enthusiastic about it, I'm sure you'll do well. The main thing is to answer any questions they have as best you can.'

I agreed to give it a try and found that it wasn't too hard after all, because I was talking about something I felt passionately about. There were never huge crowds and I didn't have to do a slick, professional presentation. It was a relief to get out of the house and to have a new interest in life, something that was worthwhile and stimulating. It helped to lift my spirits at a time when things were very difficult at home, and it wasn't long before I was wondering if there was a way I could get Allen involved in the charity. Maybe that would help him to engage with life a bit more.

The impetus had to come from him, though. He can be very stubborn and I knew I wouldn't be able to force him to do anything he didn't want to. I let him play with Ferdy and I chatted about what I was doing at Canine Partners and I left the ball in his court, so to speak.

CHAPTER SEVENTEEN

Allen

When Sandra started as a puppy walker and Ferdy came to live with us, I didn't pay much attention at first. I'd always liked dogs in the past: my mum kept Yorkshire terriers and my granddad had Labradors, but there was no way I could have been a puppy walker myself because I couldn't even look after myself, never mind take responsibility for a dog.

One day in October 1997, about a month after Sandra started going to Canine Partners, for reasons I've never found out, the morning bus didn't come to take me to day care. I waited and waited but there was no sign and Sandra was getting impatient.

'It's my puppy class day today,' she said, 'and I'm blowed if you're going to make me miss it.'

She loaded me into the car and drove me down to the converted chicken shed that Canine Partners used as a headquarters. I wheeled myself off into a corner feeling irritated by the bustle and noise level in the room.

A few people shouted, 'Hello!' and a woman called Tessa came over to try and make me join in.

'Just clap your hands, and see if you can make a puppy come to you,' she suggested.

I shook my head and snarled something bad-tempered and she soon backed off and left me on my own.

The class began. Some bowls were being placed on the ground and one by one the dogs had to go and pick up their own bowl and take it to their puppy walker. Treats were placed in the bowls but the dogs had to wait until they were given permission before eating them. I soon lost interest and just sat frowning, annoyed with the bus driver who had forgotten to come for me. I didn't particularly like the day centre but I liked sticking to my routine.

Out of the corner of my eye, I noticed that a yellow Lab kept turning round to look at me, and after a while it broke away from the crowd and came over towards me. I could see it was limping slightly but I didn't feel any sympathy. At least it could limp. I couldn't even do that any more.

When it drew close to me, it ducked down, picked something up from the floor and deposited it on my lap. It looked me in the eye, its tail wagging, obviously waiting for a response.

I didn't even glance down to see what it had brought me. Didn't this dog realize I wanted to be left on my own?

The puppies were used to getting a reward when they completed a task properly, so this Lab looked puzzled when it got nothing from me. It gazed round the room and noticed some units that were set out to look like supermarket shelves with different goods on them: tins of soup, bread, biscuits, cereal.

The Lab went over, picked something off the shelf, brought it back and dropped it in my lap. It stared up at me again, waiting for praise, but still I didn't respond. Just leave me alone, I was thinking. Give me a break!

That puppy wasn't giving up, though. He went back to the shelves and picked up another item, and I began to watch him. Mild irritation turned to amusement as he dropped a soup tin on my lap then immediately turned to go and get something else.

He had my attention now as he trotted back and forwards bringing more and more items; all of them were deposited on my lap until there was a huge, teetering pile.

Finally, I looked down and the sight of all these foods, wobbling and about to capsize on to the floor, was hilarious. I found my lips stretching into a smile for the first time in ages. My face muscles hurt with the unaccustomed movement.

'Good boy!' I whispered, and a pair of big brown eyes looked eagerly up into mine. What a handsome dog, I thought. He had a large, teddy-bear head and a very gentle expression. 'Aren't you lovely?'

'I see you've met Endal,' a well-spoken woman said. 'I think he's taken a shine to you.' She stretched out her hand. 'Judith Turner – I'm Endal's puppy parent.'

I hesitated then shook her hand. A packet toppled from my lap to the floor. 'Allen Parton,' I stuttered self-consciously. I really hated my stutter.

'Yes, I know. You're Sandra's husband, aren't you?'

I nodded, embarrassed that I didn't remember her, but she didn't seem to mind.

She carried all the goods from my lap back to the shelves and I took the opportunity to lean down and give Endal's tummy a rub underneath his red assistance jacket. I later found out that was his favourite place to be rubbed. He looked up at me with such a happy, trusting look that something in my stomach turned over. He really was the handsomest dog I'd ever come across and it was touching that he'd singled me out like that without any encouragement.

From then on, I started asking Sandra if I could come along to Canine Partners with her more often. I was curious to see what they were up to and in particular whether Endal would remember me, but at the same time something in me resisted it. What a big waste of time! It wasn't going to get me walking again or bring back my memory, was it? But every time I arrived Endal would come bounding over to see me, his big eyes gazing up at me from beside my chair, and I suppose I would be looking out for him as well. He was a very nice, very entertaining dog and I found myself thinking about him a lot in my idle moments.

Back at home I started paying more attention to Ferdy, testing him on the skills he was supposed to be learning, such as picking things up from the floor and bringing them to me.

He seemed to enjoy the extra attention. I began carrying a pocketful of doggy treats so I could reward both him and Endal, and that made me even more popular.

It got to the stage when Sandra said, 'Allen, you're going to have to back off with Ferdy. I'm supposed to be his trainer and the one he takes orders from, but he's starting to listen more to you.'

If I'm honest, I was secretly quite pleased about this, but what I didn't realize was that it jeopardized Ferdy's training. There has to be one person in charge and that has to be their trainer, in other words Sandra. By this stage, Ferdy seemed to think he was working for me but he was too young to do that and it wasn't healthy for him. Sandra chatted to Tessa, the head trainer, who agreed that it was a problem, but once the bond between Ferdy and me was established at home it was too hard to readjust the dynamic, so Tessa eventually decided that Ferdy would have to go to someone else to complete his training.

Tessa and Sandra discussed the fact that I was responding to the dogs, and asked me if I would like to be assigned an assistance dog of my own, but I was adamant I didn't want that. I didn't want to be labelled as 'disabled'. I didn't think I needed a dog to help me with anything.

Sandra tried to talk me into it. 'Allen, think of the extra freedom it would give you. You'd be able to go out to the shops on your own without worrying about whether or not you'll get knocked over when you step out into the road.'

That was something I couldn't do at the time, because I seemed to have lost my ability to judge the speed at which cars travelled. When I stood at a roadside and saw a car coming, I didn't know how quickly it would reach me, and so I'd become too nervous to cross on my own.

'It would mean you could stay at home on your own if you didn't feel like going to the day centre,' she continued.

At that time I couldn't be left alone because I could be a danger to myself. I'd put the gas on and forget about it, so a strong gust of wind could cause a fire that burned the house down. If I fell out of my chair and banged my head, I could be stuck there for hours till Sandra got home again.

'And if you dropped something and couldn't reach it, the dog could get it for you so you wouldn't have to be dependent on the kids or me the whole time,' she finished.

These arguments were all tempting, but I still resisted being pigeonholed as a disabled person. I clung to the hope that one day I would be completely fine again. My brain would heal, I would walk and talk fluently and get my memory back as good as new.

'Don't want a dog,' I snapped.

'What if you could have Endal as a pet rather than an assistance dog?' she suggested one day. 'He might not pass the tests to be an assistance dog because of the lameness in his right front leg, but he's a bright dog and he'll need a home.'

I hesitated. 'What about Ferdy?'

'Ferdy's being rehomed, and I'm getting a new puppy to train – Gracie, a sixteen-week-old golden retriever. The problem is that maybe the same thing will happen again and Gracie will think she's working for you rather than me if you don't have a dog of your own. So you'd be doing everyone a favour if you took Endal. They'd both come into the house at the same time so there'll be no established hierarchy. What do you think?'

I considered the idea and could see that us having a dog each could work. But still something in me resisted it. I found it very hard to make any decisions at all at that time – even simple things like whether it was cold enough to warrant putting a sweater on in the morning, or whether I wanted grated cheese on my pasta. I was nervous of making the wrong decision so it seemed easiest to put off the choice as long as possible. Over that Christmas we discussed it endlessly, and Sandra told me I had to make up my mind by the time the centre opened again in January.

Did I really want to be tied down by being a dog owner? Wouldn't it hamper rather than enhance my independence? It seemed like a big step to take when I was struggling to look after myself. Would I be capable of taking it out for walks and training it and all the chores that it would entail?

The main thing was that I didn't want to be registered as disabled.

'It's only words on a piece of paper,' Sandra pointed out. 'It doesn't affect your life or what you are capable of doing.'

I didn't like to say it to her but I was thinking: What if I can walk again in future? I don't want the disability label hanging over me for ever.

I think she read my mind. 'It's not permanent. If things change, that's fine.'

As the deadline approached, I said, 'You fill out the forms then if you're so keen.'

'No, it's your project,' she replied firmly. 'If you want the dog, you do it.'

It was complicated, because I had to get a doctor's recommendation form and all sorts of paperwork, but finally I completed it and handed it in that January. Then, on the morning of 28 February 1998, we met Judith Turner in the car park outside the training centre to pick up Endal. She was in floods of tears and I remember looking at her and wondering what her problem was. I was still having trouble understanding other people's emotions. She'd been training Endal for a year, since he was a few weeks old, and had become very attached to him, recognizing that he was a quite exceptional character.

She told me a bit about Endal's background and babyhood. 'He's a pure breed,' she said. 'His granddad was one of the highest-achieving Labradors ever at Crufts, but he was the result of an accidental mating between father and daughter in the kennels, the only surviving offspring in a litter.'

Sniffing back her tears, she listed some of the things he liked: 'He's partial to a bit of cheese with his dinner. He likes sleeping with his teddy bear' – she handed over a ragged, smelly creature – 'and he's very loving. He's a great licker. I'm always losing earrings that way.'

She told me he was an intelligent puppy who learned easily and liked thinking things through and solving problems for himself. He understood a lot of human language: 'He can be dead to the world, but if you say, "I'm thinking of going for a walk soon," he'll be right there by your side within nanoseconds.'

She said that when he first came to her, he was scared of the dark and had to sleep with a dim bulb glowing.

She said he had various methods of getting attention, such as pulling the washing-up bowl out of the sink and bringing it to her.

He liked the smell of port and once he managed to open a gift pack of port and Stilton and get the cork out of the bottle, without spilling a drop. They found it standing on the table like that and realized he'd just wanted to have a sniff.

Judith had a working Labrador that she took along to shoots and she told us Endal had been as well. Gun dogs are trained to pick up any kill, which she thought was good practice for an assistance dog that has to learn to pick things up for disabled people. Perhaps as a result of his experience on shoots, she said Endal loved chasing birds. When he ran after the swallows in summer, they would swoop round and fly alongside him, so he was puzzled when he tried to do the same thing with some big seagulls on holiday in East Wittering and they just flew away. He ran into the sea and tried to chase after them, wanting to play, and Judith had to yell for ages before he came back again.

'He's a big softie,' she sobbed, tears trickling down her cheeks. 'Please take good care of him.'

I was a bit bemused by all the tears. Judith gave Endal one last cuddle and Sandra lifted him into our car, then handed

Ferdy's lead to Judith, because it had been arranged that he was going to complete his training with her. I think Sandra was quite upset saying goodbye to Ferdy as well. It was a sad moment for everyone except me.

I saw Endal watching me with an intelligent look in his eyes as if he already knew what was happening and was ready for it. He wanted to look after me. He'd been brought up to look after people in wheelchairs and now he was ready to start.

What I didn't realize at the time was that Endal was going to do far more than pick up after me. His ambitions were far greater than that.

CHAPTER EIGHTEEN

Allen

The first few weeks were difficult for Endal and me. He was almost fourteen months old and had done his basic puppy-walking training with Judith, but he hadn't done the advanced training course. They weren't sure if he was going to be capable of it, given the lameness in his right leg, and were just going to watch him and see.

I wasn't sure that I would be capable of looking after a puppy, and Sandra had made it very clear that I had to do everything myself – but in fact, Endal made it easy. Judith had given me the little tin bowl he ate his dinner from and at mealtimes he would pick it up from the kitchen floor and bring it to me, as a kind of nudge. If we went out for a walk, I hooked him onto my wheelchair and he trotted along obediently beside it. Even if I let him off the leash, he never went far, always keeping an eye on me in case it was time to go home again. In the early days, he was showing me what to do, rather than the other way round.

Maybe it was because Endal had health problems, just as I did, that he managed to get through to me on an emotional level. Before he'd arrived, I just felt a kind of numbness, but he opened the door by doing little things that made me happy. The first time I threw a ball for him and he brought it back again, I knew we had a connection that didn't require communication. I liked it when he put his front paws up on my lap so that I could give him a hug. He was reaching out to me and all I had to do was respond.

After that, Endal's training was something I did instinctively. I'd put an object on the floor and say, 'Look! Look!' then ask him to bring it to me. Next time maybe I would hide it. He seemed to know intuitively what I wanted so I didn't follow any formal training methods. But I would only give a treat when a command was carried out correctly. If Endal was giving me something but just left it on the side of the wheelchair, that wouldn't do. I'd put it back down again, and he'd have to keep trying until he placed it squarely in my lap, and then he got his treat.

Sandra was learning how to be an instructor at the time and she used to come home and criticize the way I treated Endal. She said I shouldn't let him put his paws up on my lap, and that I was giving him too many treats, and I felt as though everything I did was wrong. It didn't help the atmosphere in our house, which had been volatile beforehand.

'He's my dog and I'll do it my way,' I snapped.

'You'll spoil him and he'll be no use to anyone,' she replied.

Endal had to be retrained to use our outdoor toilet area (which I call the 'pooh pit'), and that wasn't easy in a wheelchair. I had to wheel myself out into the garden in all weathers, getting the wheels covered in mud as I guided him to the exact spot. Two weeks after Endal came to live with us, we went on a day trip to Crufts and he wouldn't toilet all day because he was confused about where he was supposed to go. They had bark pits there but they obviously didn't seem right to him and it was only at a motorway service station on the way home that the floodgates opened. If we were to be able to travel outside the house, it was important that he was trained to go whenever and wherever he was let out, and that took time and patience.

On the days when Endal was limping badly he was 'off duty', but still he hovered by my chair waiting to see what he could do to help me. During his waking hours he never took his eyes off me, always alert to whatever I might need, and that devotion was touching. It can't have been very rewarding for him in those early months because I rarely spoke, so he wasn't getting any praise or interaction. It was a silent world, not much fun for a young dog.

One day I had crossed my legs by using my hands to pull my right leg across the left. As soon as Endal noticed, he bustled over and nudged my legs uncrossed again because as far as he was concerned that was the way they were meant to be. It's important for assistance dogs to be able to move your limbs back on to the wheelchair if they fall off, and Endal had just decided that my legs being crossed didn't look right to him so he fixed it.

I tested him by crossing my legs again and once more he nudged them back straight. As often as I crossed them, he would uncross them again. His persistence and dedication to duty made me laugh.

Another time, I was sitting downstairs when I rubbed my chin and realized I had forgotten to shave that morning. I decided to ask Sandra or one of the kids to go upstairs and get my electric razor so I could do a quick tidy-up, but I had one of my all-too-frequent lapses of memory and couldn't think of the word 'razor'. Cursing to myself, I kept fingering my chin in case that triggered my memory.

Endal had been watching, and suddenly he leaped up, ran out of the door and up the stairs, then returned a minute later and dropped the razor on to my lap.

Good grief! I thought, too stunned at first to remember to reward him with a doggy treat. That was extraordinary!

I told Sandra about it and she was surprised too, because reading my home-made sign language obviously wasn't something that had been covered in Endal's training. She was concerned that he shouldn't try to do too much, which could exacerbate his lameness, but she was reckoning without Endal's enthusiasm. If there was anything at all he could do for me he wanted to do it, whether there was a reward in it for him or not, and whether his legs were hurting or not.

He quickly learned more signs I invented and could soon fetch my hat for me if I patted the top of my head, my coat if

I patted the left side of my chest, his 'puppy in training' coat if I patted the right side of my chest, or my wheelchair gloves if I touched my hands. Right from the start, if I dropped something he picked it up for me straight away, and generally he began to make my life in the house much easier.

I kept a rucksack on the back of my wheelchair in which I put anything I might need. However, the lack of sensation in the right side of my body meant that when I stretched round to reach into it my brain didn't tell me what I was feeling with my fingers. I might as well have been plunging them into a bowl of jelly. I spent some time training Endal to retrieve items from the rucksack for me and that was a huge help: he could get my wallet, keys, gloves, hat or mobile phone, in response to either spoken commands or sign language. I loved teaching him new skills because he picked them up easily and never forgot, even when we'd only done something once or twice.

While I was sleeping, Endal kept watch over me, opening one eye from time to time to check I was still in the bed. Occasionally I suffered from spasms that made my legs start kicking out and when this happened I'd go and sleep on the sofa downstairs so as not to disturb Sandra. Endal would follow and find a spot in the sitting room so I was never out of his sight, even though he loved his bed upstairs. His duty was 24/7 and he wouldn't dream of letting me down.

As soon as he saw any signs that I was awake in the morning, he would jump up to lick my face. I might keep my eyes closed if I fancied a lie-in but Endal always seemed to be able to tell if I was awake; there was no fooling him. Next he would pull over my wheelchair using a little cord attached to it that we called a 'tuggie'. When I got to the toilet, he would push the loo seat up for me – although Sandra complained that like a typical male he never put it down again. He could help to fetch clothes for me to get dressed, and when we got downstairs to the kitchen he would bring the cereal packet out of the cupboard for me, by using the tuggie attached to the handle to pull the door open. Soon virtually everything in our house had a tuggie tied on to it. Then the minute the post came through the letterbox, Endal skidded out into the hall to pick it up and bring it to me; no more arguments about whom it was for – he always brought everything straight to me!

When we went out, Endal was very good at walking by the side of the chair. He had great road sense and would sit down on the kerb to stop me making the wrong decision and moving out into oncoming traffic. Only once did I doubt his abilities, when he stopped halfway across a road and paused to pick something up off the tarmac.

'Come on,' I hissed, tugging at his lead, worried that a car might come. When we got to the other side, Endal dropped a pound coin in my lap. He'd seen it lying there and thought it was the kind of thing he should pick up for me. It was actually one of the first early indications that I had a dog who wasn't just unquestioningly obedient but could actually think for himself.

The more challenges I set for him, the more he managed. You could tell that he enjoyed his job. Learning new skills was a game, and if he did it right he got a reward at the end.

I taught him some fun things as well. He would bark if I said, 'Bark!' or roll over on the ground when I circled my finger, or kiss me on the mouth if I asked him to. Other dogs might manage to offer a paw when there's a treat on offer but Endal would do anything I asked for the fun of it (not that he ever turned down a treat, of course).

My relationship with Endal became the focus of my day. I wanted to be with him the whole time, either petting him or playing with him or testing him on his skills. It was the centre of my life.

'You're in a good mood,' Sandra said when she got home from Canine Partners one day, a couple of months after Endal arrived. 'What have you been up to?'

'Look!' I said, and showed her how Endal would roll over on demand.

She laughed and called Liam and Zoe to watch. Endal was happy to perform again and soon had them all laughing. He had a natural clown's instinct and seemed to like an audience.

'Why don't you do the Canine Partners training course and learn all the advanced skills?' Sandra asked. 'I'm pretty sure Endal could pass the exam.'

I thought it sounded like a good idea, so I applied to go on their residential course in May 1998. It was usually two weeks long but I only had to do a week because I already knew all the basics about grooming and feeding.

It was fairly easy stuff that Endal had to do on the course: walking with the wheelchair, retrieving objects, coming when called. I had to learn all the proper commands, and this was taxing for me with my dodgy memory. I wrote lists and stuck them up all over the place to help with my swotting and fortunately I scraped by during the tests on the last day.

One of the tests involved teaching your dog a new skill. For us, it was entering and leaving a room. Endal had to open the door for me to get through and then pull it shut behind me. There was a tuggie attached to the door handle to make it easier for him. He'd never done this before and for some reason he pulled the door shut leaving himself inside the room. He was still a very young dog and it was quite a difficult trick to master.

We tried several times and Endal kept shutting the door with himself inside the room until I came up with a plan. As I wheeled myself out, I dropped my hankie on the floor, so Endal followed me out in order to pick up the hankie, and then he could push the door shut from the outside. The testers saw what I was doing but we got away with it.

In another part of the test, Endal and I were secretly watched as we travelled around Chichester facing different challenges. One of them was getting into and out of a lift in the local Marks & Spencer. Now, Endal and I had been there before and somehow he had worked out that when we wanted to get in he could stop the lift door closing by sticking his nose into the little laser beam at floor level. As soon as he did it, the doors opened again.

He also figured out that with this particular lift there was a bit of reflective glass at floor level and if he nudged it with his nose it would summon the lift from another floor without me having to press the button. I think this particularly impressed the trainers who were watching us at the time.

I had to make Endal lie down on the pavement outside M&S and wait for me while I went round a corner and out of sight. People hidden in the crowd kept an eye on him to make sure he stayed down, despite all the shoppers milling around, and he managed it just fine.

All in all, we passed the test with flying colours and I was really proud of him. There was a graduation ceremony on the last day of the course, with about six or seven other dogs who had passed. All the puppy walkers came along, as well as the disabled people who were taking on the dogs, and Judith Turner gave me a lovely album of photos of Endal as a puppy.

I was very proud that day. It was the first time I had achieved anything at all since I got back from the Gulf War. To think that I'd hesitated about taking on the responsibility of a dog! I'd had no idea how fulfilling it could be. I loved the independence it gave me from Sandra, the fact that I could get ready in the morning without her help and go out to the shops on my own. I felt as though I was less of a burden and, with Endal's help, I even managed to do bits and pieces of housework and contribute to the running of the household.

After he passed the advanced training course, Endal and I began to accompany Sandra to events where she was giving talks to publicize Canine Partners, and we would do little demonstrations of his skills – picking things up for me, uncrossing my legs or fetching his bowl. Then one day we were at a fête and Endal had been jumping up and showing off what he could do when he suddenly went very lame. I could tell putting any weight at all on his front legs gave him a lot of pain, and he was leaning to one side as well.

Sandra lifted him into the car and we drove him straight to the vet, who said he needed complete rest for several weeks. No jumping up, no climbing stairs, no going out for walks, just enforced bed rest. But that was easier said than done. Back at the house, Endal wouldn't stop following me about. We shut him in the kitchen instead of letting him come upstairs when we went to bed for the night, and he registered his protest by becoming very naughty. He jumped up on the work surface and took a carton of rabbit food out of a cupboard and started eating it, so it spilled everywhere. We reckon he got through about 2.5 kilos, because everything he passed for the next two weeks looked like a health food bar!

Another time when he was left alone in the kitchen he capsized the swing bin and got his head stuck through the lid, which could have been very dangerous. Basically he was objecting to being rested and having a fit of temper. The problem was he needed complete rest for his legs to improve, so reluctantly we had to agree to put him in kennels.

We took him to the charity's kennels, where he could be kept still in a small area with a rubber mat on the floor. Without space to run around, he was like a bear with a sore head. He couldn't understand why I was doing this to him, and lay there whining and chewing his rubber mat to pieces. You can't explain to an eighteen-month-old dog that it's for their own good.

I remember that while he was in kennels I went with Sandra to a graduation ceremony in which a number of other dogs were made official assistance dogs, and I missed Endal badly. There was an aching in my chest, I missed him so much. I withdrew into myself again and didn't want to talk to anyone there or join in with the events. It was as though a part of me had been torn away. I hadn't realized how important the companionship he offered was becoming to me, never mind all the help he gave me.

After he'd been in kennels for two weeks, Heather, one of the training centre managers, took Endal to the vet for another check-up, then came round to tell me the verdict.

'I'm afraid it's bad news, Allen. Endal isn't any better and we don't know what to do. It may be that he'll always have this problem and will need proper care and attention, which would mean he can't be a full working dog.'

That struck fear into me. I was lame myself and I couldn't have a dog that was lame. It could inhibit my recovery if I had to go back to being a prisoner in my own home because I was looking after him. I needed a dog I could take to the shops, that would increase rather than decrease my mobility and independence.

'Take him back then,' I blurted out, and turned away from her. 'I don't want him.' My throat tightened and I felt like crying but I was too stubborn to back down. I wheeled my chair out of the room and shut the door behind me, leaving her to let herself out.

CHAPTER NINETEEN

Sandra

All the staff at Canine Partners had been hoping that Allen would apply for Endal. When he was a puppy, there was some doubt whether Endal would ever pass the test to be a full working assistance dog because he had a condition called osteochondritis, or OCD, in his front elbow joints. This means that as the dog develops, the cartilage doesn't turn into bone as it is meant to, causing swelling in the joint and intermittent lameness.

Endal wouldn't have been able to work for someone who didn't have much upper body strength because they would need a dog that could jump up on its hind legs to fetch things for them. Allen has always had very good upper body strength though, so we thought they were a good match. Apart from anything else, there seemed to be a strong attraction between them. As soon as Allen arrived at a puppy class,

Endal would leave Judith's side and go over to see him. There was a definite spark there.

When Allen took Endal to do the residential training course, I worried that he might be grouchy and demanding with the staff the way he was with me at home, but they said he was fine. He was, however, a bit arrogant at first, thinking that he knew it all because he'd had his dog for three months already, so one day they taught him a lesson by 'stealing' Endal away from him.

'Didn't he explode when you did that?' I asked. 'He'd go berserk if I did that at home.'

'No,' they said, 'he took it all in good spirit.'

I was astonished to hear this. I couldn't imagine him being the butt of a joke without growling at someone, but it seemed that he was regaining his ability to laugh at himself. That was one of the moments when I really sensed things were changing for the better. When I thought about it, I realized he'd been getting more fun-loving at home as well. There had been a few times when we'd had a laugh together, usually because of something to do with the dogs.

It was a huge setback when Endal went badly lame. He had to go for complete rest in kennels, and he hated it and barked so much that he lost his voice. When he came out, I knew there was still a question mark over his fitness but I was very upset when I heard from Heather that Allen was refusing to take him back again. I couldn't believe it! I thought Allen really cared about that dog and loved the independence Endal gave him, and here he was, ready to throw it all away.

It would have been a giant step backwards – for Allen himself and for us as a couple.

'Maybe they haven't bonded as well as we thought?' Heather suggested.

'But they have!' I insisted. Then I thought about it. 'The only reservation Allen has expressed to me is about the fact that Endal isn't *his* dog. He's worried that if things go wrong, for example if Endal gets so lame that he can't work, you might come and take him away again.' All Canine Partners dogs were owned by the charity, not the individuals they worked for.

'We could reassure him about that. I'm sure we could come to an agreement that Endal is his for as long as he wants him.'

'That might make a difference,' I said. 'Leave it with me. I'll talk to him tonight.'

As I drove home, I became more and more determined that I wasn't going to let Allen throw away all the progress we'd made in the last few months. I couldn't go back to the silence, the bad temper and the dependence of the man he'd been before Endal came into our lives. The thought was unbearable.

I waited until Allen and I were in bed that night and I gave him a real talking-to.

'What's this nonsense I hear that you're refusing to take Endal back?'

'He's lame. He can't help me any more.' Allen was sullen and I knew he could get very obstinate when he was in this kind of mood.

'Will you stop being so selfish!' I shouted. 'Try thinking of someone else apart from yourself for a change. That dog needs you, and he's done a lot for you, and you're prepared to just throw it all away.'

'I can't have a limpy dog,' he muttered.

'*Why* can't you?' I demanded. 'Why not give Endal a chance to get better, just as everyone else is giving you a chance? What are you so scared of?'

He didn't say anything.

'If you're worried that Canine Partners might take him away, that's not a problem. They've said that Endal can be your dog for life, whether he can work or not.'

Still he said nothing.

'You think about it, Allen. That dog didn't ask to have joint problems any more than you asked to be brain-damaged in a car accident. Just bear in mind that I will be furious with you if you throw away this opportunity through your stubbornness and self-centredness.'

He didn't say any more, but I could hear that he lay awake for quite a while and I hoped he was thinking about what I'd said.

The next morning, I didn't help him to get up. I left him to pull his own chair over to the bed, get his own clothes and then stretch to get his own breakfast cereal out of the cupboard. I wanted him to remember how much tougher life was for him without a dog.

As we were eating, Allen asked, 'What time are you leaving?'

'About half nine. Why?'

'I think I'll come with you to the training centre,' he said quietly.

'Fine.' I tried not to smile. It looked as though my words had had an effect.

As soon as we arrived, I saw Allen looking round for Endal.

'Where is he?' he asked Heather.

'Endal? He's back at the kennels.'

'I've changed my mind. Do you think I could have him back, please?'

He even said 'please'. I felt like punching the air in triumph.

Heather smiled and said, 'Of course you can.' She went on to explain that they were happy for Endal to remain with him as a pet in the worst-case scenario that he couldn't work, and they went off to have a chat together. Later that day we picked up Endal and brought him home again.

For the first few days, I was watching them closely and I noticed that Allen was very affectionate with Endal, cuddling and patting him and giving him constant attention. It was very sweet to watch, actually. When you live with someone it can be a while before you are aware they are changing, although someone who sees them less frequently might notice straight away, but I definitely felt that Allen was happier than I had seen him since before the accident. Happier, and easier to live with.

Endal was utterly devoted to Allen and very focused on getting him whatever he needed. When Allen couldn't remember a word and used sign language instead, some dogs would have given up but Endal kept trying until he worked out what was wanted. He never gave up. Some dogs will pick up a pencil from the floor once, twice, maybe three times and then they think: I'm not picking that up again. Endal would have kept doing it as long as Allen kept dropping the pencil, even if that was a hundred times. He was totally consistent and totally reliable.

When I went out and left Allen at home with Endal, I knew he was safe. If anything had happened, for example if Allen had fallen out of the chair, Endal would have alerted the neighbours straight away. If they went down to the shops together, Endal had good road sense and stopped him rolling out into oncoming traffic. It was a huge weight off my mind to be able to leave him without worrying. Even though Allen stopped going to the Horizon Centre once he had a puppy to look after, I still had a great deal more freedom.

Allen and Endal were great buddies, totally focused on each other. It was a real boys' club and they could be quite exclusive: Endal really didn't want to take orders from me, and Allen certainly didn't. It was funny for me seeing my husband getting so close to someone else in a way that he wasn't close to me, but I wasn't jealous for a second. My over-whelming emotion was relief that Allen's mental outlook was getting so much healthier. I felt a stirring of optimism for the first time in seven long years.

CHAPTER TWENTY

Allen

After Endal's problem with lameness, we had to take it very easy when he came back to stay with me. He couldn't run for a ball and he wasn't supposed to jump up on his hind legs, which was hard because we used to like having a cuddle when he put his paws up on my lap. He was only allowed a minute's walk the first day, then two minutes, then three, and it was several months before he was able to come out of the house and down to the shops with me. He couldn't run and retrieve a ball or be let off the lead to play. It was particularly important that we kept his weight under control, so I put him on a raw food diet of fresh meat and cereal, as well as the doggy treats I offered whenever he did something especially clever. He was weighed once a week and I had strict instructions that if he went over 31 kilos he was to be given smaller portions until his weight went back down again.

Even stuck indoors, Endal was a very responsive companion, and we started playing lots of games together. He loved his kong, a hardened rubber toy on a string that I would put a biscuit inside. He would swing it around as if it was a wild creature he was trying to subdue and he'd chew away at it until he had wrestled the treat out of the middle. If I got hold of it or tried to yank it out of his mouth, he would run off round the room with it before bringing it back again. Sometimes I hid it and he had to find it. We got a little routine going between us.

Another game he enjoyed was hide and seek. If he was in the garden, I'd sneak into the house and find a hiding place – not easy with a wheelchair in a small house – then wait as he came scurrying in to find me. It never took him long and he'd be overjoyed and bark happily when he saw me again. I started hiding behind bushes when we went out for a walk but he'd always find me within thirty seconds.

Endal wasn't really supposed to climb the stairs at first because of his lame front legs, but he was so unhappy if I left him downstairs that I gave in and let him come up at nighttime only. His bed was just by my side of the bed in our bedroom, and it was made up of a king-size duvet folded several times and stuffed inside a single duvet cover, with a big, smelly doggy cushion on top. His favourite position for sleeping was on his back with his legs splayed wide. I liked to watch him while he wriggled in his sleep in the midst of a doggy dream, probably about chasing cats or birds or squirrels.

I think his early experience as a gun dog influenced Endal to an extent, because once he was allowed off the leash he liked nothing better than charging after small animals and birds. He would never have harmed them; he just wanted to play. We had rabbits at home and he would let them climb all over him without as much as a 'wuff'. And I once saw him sharing his food with a magpie in the garden, which I can't imagine many other dogs would do.

When he was off the lead in an open space, Endal would set off at a run to try and catch any birds, squirrels or cats he caught sight of but his training was such that if I called him to 'stop' then he'd do so immediately. If he's on the lead, I can feel the tension when he notices a small animal, but he would never pull too hard and risk me falling out of the chair.

He was keen on eating any cat pooh he came across on our walks but a doggy expert told me that it is full of protein and good for them to eat so I didn't stop him, even though his breath was horrible afterwards. And, like most Labs I've come across, he loved rolling in fox pooh and impregnating his entire coat with the scent. It's the Chanel No. 5 of the doggy world, as far as I can see.

At Christmas, when Sandra brought the turkey home from the butchers and put it in the fridge, she would turn round and Endal would be sitting there with his tongue hanging out. He could smell a turkey at a hundred paces. It became a standard ritual that she would open the fridge door just a fraction and, whatever room Endal had been in, she would look round to see him sitting right there looking up at her expectantly, tongue hanging out. Of course, we had to give him some pieces of turkey on Christmas Day and it proved to be a hot favourite.

Endal has antennae for biscuits as well. He can smell one at fifty paces. At the Canine Partners training centre, he always used to nose around an old corner cabinet and we couldn't figure out why until it was moved one day and we found a manky bit of leftover biscuit underneath. He had been able to smell it and it really used to bug him until he could finally claim it.

He would never steal food; he was too well trained for that. The only time Endal was really naughty, that I can remember, is when I took him for a walk around a nearby lake. He dived straight into the water and despite all my calling, offering of treats and then angry shouting, he didn't come out for hours. He just loved swimming. His tail is slightly flattened like an otter's and he's a very strong swimmer. It's the only time he's abandoned me when we've been out, but I reckon it might be good for his joints so after that occasion I usually let him have a swim whenever we were near somewhere suitable.

Gradually, over the course of a year or so, I noticed that Endal was limping less and then barely at all. Once the vet had given him the all-clear, he was able to start accompanying me to events designed to promote the charity. He always liked going out and about and meeting new people, especially children, and I enjoyed my days out as well just for the break in my normal routine.

We started to become well known in the Clanfield area. When we went into the grocer's shop, I would point to the goods I wanted on the shelves and Endal would pick them up for me, much to the other customers' amazement. I always felt that we had to buy whatever he picked up rather than leave a saliva-soaked package for the next customer to find, but the staff were very understanding and happy to have us there. The chemist didn't have disabled access at that time so I would wait outside while Endal went in to pick up my prescription. At the post office, he could post letters in the letterbox or push forms into the service tray under the glass security panel. And if we stopped for a pint in the pub on the way home, Endal would jump up at the bar and hand my wallet to the barman so he could take out the money for my drink. All of these things would have been difficult or impossible for me before because I couldn't stretch far out of the chair. We became a familiar sight around the village and everyone used to stop to say hello and pat Endal.

I hadn't ever learned to drive before the accident and it was out of the question afterwards because of the brain damage I'd suffered, but once the local buses got a disabled ramp I could travel on them throughout the neighbourhood. We had a routine. While I wheeled myself up the ramp, Endal would take my wallet to the driver so he could extract the right money. Endal would then tear off the ticket and bring it and the wallet back to me while I parked myself in the wheelchair space. It worked like clockwork.

Having Endal made my confidence grow in all sorts of ways. Apart from playing with him, I spent most of my time learning new functions on the computer. Out of curiosity I decided to take it apart and figure out how everything worked. Computers are basically just a mechanical box with a power supply and lots of microchips and they hold the same kind of fascination for me as Lego had done when I was a kid. I've always liked problem-solving, and this gave me something to focus on.

I remembered a missile system I'd worked on back in the 1980s that kept going wrong because it saw the horizon as a target and locked on to it. It was tracking along the horizon and they couldn't unlock it, and we had to rewrite the program to solve that problem. That's the kind of work I used to do, and I missed the technical challenges. I missed using my brain – what was left of it.

One day I saw an advert in a computer magazine for a casing that you could buy to build your own computer in. I bought it by mail order, and when it was delivered I hid it in the garage. Gradually I started buying more bits and pieces and hiding them all from Sandra. I used to disappear out there and started putting them all together, working it out through trial and error. I didn't have a monitor at first so I couldn't see if it was working properly but the lights went on and it seemed to be making the right noises. Endal barked, as if congratulating me.

I remember one of my old Navy bosses saying, 'Divide a problem into bits.' That's what you do with engineering. If a signal is coming in but the device isn't working, you look at the next bit of wire, use logic to find any faults and go through it slowly. It took a while, but finally I got my computer working all by myself. It was such a proud moment when I plugged everything in, booted up and the screen came to life.

'Sandra,' I called. 'Come and see.'

She came out to the garage but didn't seem very impressed. 'What is it?'

'I made my own computer.' I clicked on a program to show her that it worked.

'It's a bit big, isn't it? I hope you don't want to bring it into the house because there wouldn't be any room.'

I was disappointed that she wasn't more enthusiastic but I was still chuffed with myself that I had managed it. I wasn't a stupid person before the accident and, despite my memory problems, I wasn't stupid after it either.

In March 1999 I took Endal for his second visit to Crufts, where Sandra and I were helping to do talks and demonstrations at the Canine Partners stall. I was starting to say a bit more at these events, but I was very nervous about it in the early days. I knew I could talk fairly fluently but I couldn't memorize a speech, and as I didn't remember what I'd said two minutes before there was a real risk of me repeating myself. I just had to take a leap of faith and go with it. I remembered that after she left office, a famous politician who shall remain nameless once made a joke in a speech and her audience laughed, then ten minutes later she made the same joke again and a hush filled the room. I didn't want that happening to me, so I kept my presentations short and snappy. What they really wanted to see was Endal doing his stuff: nudging my leg back on to the chair when it fell off, picking up things I had dropped and so forth. Endal was a real showman and played up to an audience with impeccable timing and comic flair.

Gaby Roslin was at Crufts that year filming for a TV special and she asked if they could take some footage of Endal putting my leg back on to the chair. I was happy to oblige, but every time they moved my leg off ready to start filming, Endal would push it back on again before the cameras started rolling. Gaby was in stitches as she watched.

After the Crufts competition finished and everyone was packing up, Endal and I went to have a play in the main ring. Some spectators were sitting round the sides eating their sandwiches as we began messing around with the kong. I tugged on the kong and Endal ran off round the ring with it, then brought it back to me to tug again. We had extended our sign language so that if I circled my finger in the air, he would roll over three or four times, and he could also respond to hand signs for 'Sit', 'Wait', 'Come' and so forth, even when I was some distance away.

I signalled to Endal to run round the ring again and he set off, and I was stunned to hear the onlookers clapping. I didn't realize anyone had been watching our game, but they were laughing at his antics and seemed to be amazed at this dog who understood sign language. From across the ring I signed to Endal to roll over again, and he did. There was no hint of the lame dog of a year ago. He was playful, intelligent and a born performer.

As we were leaving, I slipped Endal's kong into the rucksack on the back of my wheelchair, knowing that he would immediately go in there to retrieve it. Sure enough, as I wheeled myself away Endal pulled out the kong again and the audience erupted into laughter.

While I was making my way back to the Canine Partners stand to find Sandra, a Crufts official came hurrying over to introduce himself.

'That was a fantastic display you did there,' he said.

'It wasn't a display. We were just playing.'

'Well, I wondered whether you would come and do it again next year as a demo? People would love to watch you two together.'

What could I say? I was delighted to be asked.

More and more, this dog was bringing fun and joy back into my life. Dogs are utterly non-judgemental so if I woke up feeling irritable one morning, while Sandra might snap back at me and storm out of the room, Endal was endlessly patient and accepting. If I was depressed, he came up on my lap for a snuggle. If my chair got stuck, he would try to clear obstacles out of the way. He was always ready to pick up whatever objects I dropped. From the moment he arrived in my life he gave me unqualified, unconditional love that shone out of his gentle face gazing up at me by the side of my chair.

I still had frequent bad days, when the unfairness of what had happened to me was brought home. It was psychologically bruising when I heard on the news or read in the paper about British armed forces fatalities overseas. In the press it's just an unnamed soldier until the families have been informed, then there's a photo of a fresh-faced lad and maybe some tributes from colleagues, and the next day it's over for everyone else but the relatives and close friends, who have to live with it for the rest of their lives. That always used to get to me and cast my spirits down, but Endal would just nudge me with his nose and bring me his kong and remind me that at least there was one thing in life I had to be grateful for.

CHAPTER TWENTY-ONE

Sandra

Canine Partners was a small charity where everyone mucked in. Once Allen and Endal were established as a partnership, Tessa asked whether he would be prepared to come along to weekend events with me and give a demonstration of the kind of skills assistance dogs were capable of. This included things like opening cupboard doors by pulling a little tuggie cord attached to them and then taking out the object requested, or fetching an item from the backpack Allen kept on his wheelchair, or picking up something he'd dropped on the ground. Endal was a perfect dog to use for demonstrations because we knew he would get it right every time. You told him what you wanted and he did it without hesitation.

We agreed that when he came to these demonstrations, Allen could answer direct, simple questions from the audience, such as Endal's age, but he wouldn't have to tell any stories or talk at length. We'd work together and I'd do the chatty bits.

Right from the start, we made a good team. I was the 'straight' one who got the facts across, and Allen and Endal were the comedy showmen. We didn't rehearse our 'act' – there was no point, because Allen would have forgotten any script we came up with – but it all fell naturally into place. It was fun. I enjoyed it and I could tell that Allen did as well. He was interacting with members of the public, forgetting to be embarrassed about his stammer – although when I listened closely, I realized that was happening less and less. Another time, I noticed that his compulsive twitching was becoming much less frequent.

It was only gradually, over the months, that I noticed Allen was doing more and more of the talking at charity fundraising events. One day I stood back and listened as he spoke to a member of the audience at one of our demonstrations. He was describing the time when Endal had piled objects on his lap at the training centre, and I realized he wasn't stuttering at all and he didn't forget any of his words. What's more, he was smiling at the woman who had asked the question, and acting like a normal, sociable human being. As I watched, I got goose bumps. In the way he was chatting, I could see the friendly, gregarious man I had fallen for back in that night-club in Haslemere – the man I thought I'd lost for ever. It was a wonderful sight.

Where speech therapists had failed to get him speaking clearly in sentences during the seven years since his accident, it seemed that the relationship he had formed with Endal had increased his desire to communicate and had somehow helped his brain to re-form a link that had been missing. That's the only explanation I can come up with and the doctors couldn't come up with anything better.

Once he could speak more clearly, Allen began to engage with the world again. He'd chat to people we met, and although he could still be tactless and harsh his natural cheerfulness, which had been absent for the previous seven years, came back. Of course, the huge gaps in his memory still hadn't been filled in, and he still forgot the names of people he'd known for years, but I felt a real sea change in his mental outlook.

There were just a few little signs that he was beginning to think about the children and me, and to care about all the memories of us that he had lost. He asked me questions about what happened at our wedding, about the birth of the children, and about what they had been like as toddlers, and the fact that he was starting to care again made me start to fall back in love with him. I'd never fallen out of love with the man he used to be, and it all came flooding back as I recognized that person in him again.

His sense of humour had disappeared after the accident. At Headley Court he displayed a kind of black humour to deflect reality, or if he felt he was being pushed into a corner. He thought he could wriggle out of situations by telling jokes, but it wasn't the sense of humour he'd had before, and to me it frequently wasn't funny. When Endal first came to live with us Allen was still very serious and humourless, but gradually at the puppy classes he learned to laugh at himself again – and to try to make others laugh as well. The corny jokes crept back and along with them the practical jokes.

One day I was in the kitchen preparing dinner when Allen wheeled himself in with a bar of soap in his hand.

'Does this smell funny to you?' he asked, holding it out.

I bent down to smell it, and sure enough he tipped it up so I got soap on my nose. I remembered the first time he played that trick on me, back in 1982 when we'd first started dating. I laughed quickly and turned away so that he wouldn't see my tears because it would have spoiled the moment to explain it to him. It was good to see so many aspects of the old Allen coming back, but still poignant that he didn't seem to remember he'd ever done that to me before.

One day, as we were driving along a country lane, I thought I ran over a cat. I'd seen it dashing in front of the car but when I looked in the mirror it wasn't visible on the road behind. 'Maybe it's got sucked up into the engine,' I worried out loud. I braked sharply and got out to have a look. Just as I opened the bonnet, Allen made a loud miaowing sound, like a cat being tortured, and I just about jumped out of my skin. I fell for his wind-ups every time.

One of the best things for me was that he began to bond with the children, through playing with the puppies together. They'd loved having dogs from the moment Ferdy first arrived to live with us. Although Endal really only took orders from Allen, Liam and Zoe would fall about laughing as they watched him perform all the skills he had mastered and would whoop with delight every time he barked on demand or rolled over in response to Allen circling his finger.

Endal naturally had a range of different barks and Allen had been teaching him to produce them on demand. An expert once told me that the normal dog has only eight voice patterns but Endal has at least twenty, all with different meanings.

There was a little bark he used with children, a soft, gentle mouth bark that makes people laugh because it sounds funny coming from such a big dog. There's his 'Hello' bark, which always surprises people: if you say 'Hello' to Endal, he will answer you with a kind of 'wuff' sound. There's his 'I love you' bark and his 'Turn over the TV channel bark' and his 'Can I have another treat?' bark. There's a louder and more assertive 'ruff', a hound-like 'yaowww', a full-on big bark, and many more besides.

If Allen said, 'Gentle!' he got the children's one that was almost like a coughing sound; if he said, 'Big bark!' he got the loudest one; and he had different commands for most of the others in between. He also taught him to bark whenever there was a toast to the Queen, just as a party piece!

The kids loved getting Endal to do his different barks and they often joked about his 'super-powers'.

'Can you get him to turn over the telly?' Zoe asked.

'Or can he do my homework for me?' Liam chimed in.

'He'd probably do it better than you,' Allen quipped, 'but it's you who'll have to pass the exams so you're out of luck.'

Around this period, Allen's granddad Roger was admitted to hospital. He was ninety-odd and very sprightly but he fell in his bathroom one night, broke his femur and then his kidneys started to fail. Allen had been very close to this granddad, his mother's father, who had been an important figure in his childhood after his dad walked out on them – but he had no memories of him from before the accident. He just knew him as a lively old man whom we visited sometimes.

We went to see Roger in hospital but by the time we got there he was in a coma, and several family members were gathered round the bed because the end was near. If Allen had recalled all the closeness they'd had in his childhood, he'd probably have been very upset. As it was, he lightened the mood of the gathering by suggesting we send out for beer and pizza. Everyone was hungry so they agreed and we sat by the old man's bedside with an almost festive atmosphere, munching our pizzas. It may sound odd but it's exactly what Roger would have wanted. He had an amazing sense of humour – it's probably where Allen got his from – and I think he would have been tickled by that scene round his hospital bed.

I was delighted with the way Allen dealt with the situation that night. He couldn't relate to the grief people were feeling, but he sensed it and was respectful of it. There were no inappropriate comments at all. I remembered when he had refused to come to baby Alice's funeral back in the bad old days. We seemed to have come a long way since then. His memory hadn't returned but he was looking outside himself and learning to be more considerate towards other people.

I felt more relaxed and happy at home, and my spirits were also lifted by the work I was doing at Canine Partners. Every single dog that came through the door had a different personality but they all loved learning the skills and getting them right. Some of them were so wayward they drove you to despair, while others picked everything up straight away and shone in the classes. Some were calm while others were skittish and yappy, and yet more were clingy and affectionate.

As well as helping at the groups for puppy walkers and their dogs, I started getting involved in the advanced training that was done when the dogs were between fourteen and eighteen months old.

Right from the beginning, puppies were taught to sit down whenever they got to a kerb, but we had to familiarize them with different kinds of kerbs: high kerbs, dropped kerbs, and those knobbly yellow ones designed for blind people. When they went out for walks, we'd place a group of other dogs in the corner of the field to test them. Of course, they were interested to see what the other dogs were doing but they had to learn to stay with the person they were looking after and not run off when there was a distraction of any kind.

The puppies came to live at the training centre when they were doing their advanced training. It was a step up and they were pushed a bit harder. The trainers were often sitting in wheelchairs as they gave the instructions and the dogs were expected to be aware where the chair was at all times because, apart from anything else, they had to make sure their feet didn't get caught under the wheels. We used chairs with very soft wheels, but still we found that a dog would only make a mistake and get a foot caught once and it would be super-careful from then on.

We taught the dogs how to put their front paws up on a wall and push a light switch with their noses, or to press the button at a pelican crossing. We taught them to open and close doors with tuggies attached to them, to pull washing out of a washing machine into a laundry basket then drag it out into the garden to be pegged on a line, and to push the foot-plates down on wheelchairs, for example when the chair has just been taken out of a car.

We taught them a typical checkout sequence for use in a supermarket. The dog should go into the aisle in front of the wheelchair then turn round to face their partner and walk backwards through the narrow space. If their partner can't reach the shop assistant, the dog should take the purse from them and jump up to hand it over so the assistant can take the correct money. They then hand it back afterwards.

The dogs learned life-saving skills tailored to the person they were going to take care of. They might be trained to get help if someone has an epileptic fit, in particular pulling out the plug if they lost consciousness in the bath. If we lay down on the floor with our eyes shut during training, they had to find another trainer, stand in front of them and bark or even grab their clothes to try and pull them over to help. We used to get them to sit in front of someone, bark and paw at their leg, but this was stopped after one dog hurt a trainer's knee during a demo when they got just a little bit too enthusiastic!

The dogs learned up to a hundred key words before they graduated as fully fledged assistance puppies. They knew all the basics, such as 'Sit', 'Down', 'Stand', 'Roll over', 'Turn around', 'Move', 'Heel', 'Side', 'Behind', 'Up'. Once they knew these, you would make the command a bit more complicated, such as 'Can you get it and bring it here?' The dog would start looking, find the object, pick it up in its mouth and bring it over. Then we would start teaching them the names of different items, such as keys, phone, purse. If all three items were lying on the floor beside each other and you said, 'Bring me the keys,' the dog had to be able to pick up the keys consistently.

We would add new words to basic commands. Once they knew 'Up', for example, we might say 'Up table', 'Up stool' or 'Up car'. This meant they would put their front legs up on the thing named. 'Jump on' meant they were to jump with all four legs. Many disabled people like to come out of their chair on to a sofa in the evening to have a cuddle with their dog, so we taught 'Jump on sofa' as one of the commands – although they were only allowed to do this when invited. The same went for 'Jump on bed'.

I came home every day and told Allen what we had been doing, and he was curious and asked lots of questions, then really listened to the answers. It was wonderful to realize that we had this new interest in common now. We started having conversations again for the first time since the accident. He asked about my day, and I asked what he and Endal had been doing, and we were communicating properly, rather than me asking how he was feeling and him telling me about his aches and pains or complaining about something the kids had done.

If anything had happened that upset me during the day, Allen listened and seemed to care. It made me feel less lonely than I had been. Our relationship was beginning to feel like a friendship, although it still wasn't a marriage – but I had no idea at that stage where it was going to take us next.

CHAPTER TWENTY-TWO

Allen

Endal had an incredible appetite for learning new skills to help me. He was always on the look-out for new ways of assisting me and would stand by watching me most of the time. If I appeared to hesitate or struggle with a task, he would move in to do what he could.

One day I went to get some money out of a cash machine. It was slightly tricky because the sun was shining on the screen, so I put the card in and then had to manoeuvre my chair to the other side to shade the keyboard so I could key in my PIN number. The machine spat my card back out before I had shifted myself back into the correct position to reach it and, without being asked, Endal jumped up and grabbed it in his mouth then turned and handed it to me.

'Wow! Good boy,' I said, and gave him a treat from my pocket. 'That was neat!'

Of course, once he saw that it earned him a treat, he was keen to repeat his new skill. When the money slid out, Endal leaped up to retrieve it before I could stop him. I took it from him rather nervously, hoping that his teeth hadn't torn any of the notes, but I needn't have worried. He was usually very gentle when picking anything up for me, and the worst that would happen was that items could be a bit slimy from his saliva.

Endal was delighted to have found a new way to assist me, so the cashpoint became part of our routine whenever we were in town. I thought I would see if he could go a step further, so one day when we arrived at the machine I put the card in Endal's mouth the right way round and he jumped up and tried to insert it in the slot. It took a bit of effort and a slight helping hand from me before he pushed it in and the machine sucked it away for processing. After that, Endal became an expert at positioning my card into all kinds of cash machines, whether they had slots on the sides or front. I admit he broke a couple of cards in his enthusiasm because he really flew at the job, but I considered it a price worth paying. I was so proud of him.

One day in the summer of 1999, we were getting cash from a machine in Havant. I was quite blasé about it by now because Endal always did it perfectly. He put the card in the slot, waited while I keyed in my PIN number and then retrieved the card and the cash for me, in return for which I gave him a doggy treat. I was just tucking the money in my wallet when I felt a hand on my shoulder.

'Excuse me,' a man's voice said. 'Did I really just see your dog using the cash machine?'

'Yes. He always does it for me.' I turned the chair round to see whom I was talking to.

'I'm a reporter for the *News of the World*. I'd be interested in running a story about this, but I wonder if you would mind getting your dog to do it again so I can watch?'

'OK,' I said. 'I'll take out another tenner.' I gave Endal my card and to the journalist's amazement he put it straight in the slot, waited for me to key in the PIN number and then retrieved the card and cash afterwards.

The journalist was clearly impressed. 'Can I take a photo of him doing it?'

'Sure.' I shrugged. 'Why not?'

Endal performed impeccably, even holding still with the card in his mouth, poised at the entrance to the slot so the journalist could get the picture he wanted. When he'd finished, Endal turned to me for his treat, as usual.

The journalist asked some questions about our relationship then said, 'Thanks very much,' and told us the article would be in the paper the following Sunday.

'You'll never guess what …' I told Sandra later, and she raised her eyebrows, as if to say: 'Whatever next?'

We bought the paper that Sunday and, sure enough, there we were on page five. It felt nice, and I was glad that Endal was getting recognition for being so special.

I had no idea what that first article was going to lead to but it seems it was noticed by a wide readership. People started mentioning it whenever Endal and I went to Canine Partners events and they'd ask me what else Endal could do.

Then, a month or so later, I got a letter through the post saying that *Dogs Today* magazine wanted to photograph Endal for a calendar they were producing for the new millennium. I didn't know anyone from *Dogs Today* at the time, and can only assume they heard about us through the *News of the World* article. The letter said that they would choose one of the twelve dogs they photographed to be their 'Dog of the Millennium'. We were given a time and a place to turn up and told there would be a doggy groomer available to spruce Endal up for his photo.

Sandra, the kids and I went to stay in a hotel in Slough with Endal the night before, then we made our way to the photographer's studio. I was excited but at the same time it felt very bizarre that we were being singled out like this.

Each dog had been allotted its own half-hour time slot. I was slightly disappointed when we went in that they decided Endal didn't need any grooming at all – he was handsome enough as he was. The photographer specialized in shooting cats and dogs, and he had a range of toys that made funny squeaky noises. When he wanted a dog to look at the camera, he just squeezed the toy beside it, and then pressed the shutter to capture the shot when they looked up. Endal was very cooperative and did whatever they asked him to. Right from the start he always liked cameras and seemed to sense what he was supposed to do with them.

After the photography, there was to be an announcement about which dog was to be the Millennium Dog. The twelve calendar dogs had been voted for by readers of *Dogs Today*, and a panel of judges was deciding the overall winner. I hadn't really paid much attention to that part of the letter; I was just happy that Endal was going to be in a calendar at all. Then a woman came over and told us that Endal was the Dog of the Millennium and I couldn't believe my ears. I thought I'd misheard, except that everyone was turning to us and clapping.

I was even more amazed when we were told that there was an award of £500, but straight away I said that the money would go to Canine Partners. Endal was their dog, and I certainly didn't intend to profit from him.

What I wasn't ready for at all was the sight that met my eyes when the doors opened. Several TV cameras and journalists appeared clutching notepads and tape recorders and microphones and everyone was shouting: 'Where's Endal?' 'How does it feel to be the Millennium Dog?' 'Can we have a shot of the two of you?' 'Look this way, please!'

I answered their questions and Endal put his front paws up on my knees as we posed for photographs. It was quite overwhelming, but at the same time I felt that Endal deserved it. He was an extraordinary dog and I was glad for him to have what I thought would be his fifteen minutes of fame. I knew there were other very talented dogs out there but it was lovely that my dog was being recognized for the eighteen months of hard work he had done for me. If that made him 'Dog of the Millennium', who was I to grumble?

There was a display of Beta dog food, because Beta were the sponsors of the Dog of the Millennium contest, so we had to get lots of photos of Endal with their display in the background. However, I think they were a bit unhappy shortly after this when someone photographed Endal picking up a tin of Butcher's dog food and passed the pictures on to their press office. Shortly afterwards, Butcher's ran a big advert on the back of the *Telegraph* using the picture, with the caption 'Is your dog as clever as a Butcher's dog?'

Next we got an invitation to be interviewed on GMTV with Eamonn Holmes and Fiona Phillips. Everyone at the Canine Partners training centre was jumping up and down asking us to get their autographs, which I did. I don't remember much about that first TV appearance. I was nervous that I would make a fool of myself when it was my turn to talk, maybe repeating myself or stammering over a word, but in fact Sandra did most of the talking and I just answered a few quick queries, in the same way we did at Canine Partners presentations. Endal sat sagely on the sofa, looking around with interest at all the camera equipment and sound men with mics scurrying across the floor. He barked when asked to and behaved impeccably.

The Canine Partners management were delighted about the Dog of the Millennium award and the publicity it generated. Not long afterwards they invited me to become a trustee of the charity, which was an incredible boost to my confidence, still dented by the way the job at *Collingwood* had turned out. Maybe there was useful work I could do despite my faulty memory, damaged cognitive powers and unresponsive legs. Maybe I wasn't ready for the scrapheap just yet. I decided to devote myself to raising money for them as best I could, using Endal's media profile if that helped.

My life seemed to have turned round from misery and gloom to pride and achievement in just a couple of years. Where psychologists and therapists and doctors had all failed, a very talented Labrador had changed my world and made my life worth living again.

CHAPTER TWENTY-THREE

Sandra

Allen and I have no idea who nominated Endal for the Millennium Dog of the Year award, but the picture that was entered was the one from the *News of the World* article about his cashpoint skills. We all stayed the night in Slough before the photo shoot – the children came as well – then made our way to the studio early next morning for our half-hour slot with the photographer. Suddenly it was announced that Endal was the overall winner and we were overwhelmed by the number of journalists who appeared out of nowhere. Allen coped with it amazingly well but I remember feeling very shy when it was my turn to be interviewed. Liam was like me but Zoe turned out to be a real media junkie, always happy to be in the limelight.

That evening, we were on the BBC *Six O'Clock News* and the ITV evening news and when the papers came out the next morning we were on the front cover of all of them, which was a peculiar feeling. I suppose I'd never thought of Endal as particularly unusual before because all the dogs we trained at Canine Partners were exceptional, but I must admit that I didn't know of any others who could use a cashpoint machine.

I felt very shy when we went on GMTV, but Eamonn Holmes was so nice that I soon forgot there were millions of viewers watching and just spoke directly to him. If I tuned out the cameras and sound crew, I could pretend it was just like doing another presentation to raise funds and find new puppy walkers for Canine Partners.

I was still puppy walking myself. By the time Endal won Dog of the Millennium, Gracie had passed her advanced training and moved on to live with a wheelchair-bound QC, where she leads a very starry, high-powered life, moving in royal circles on occasion.

After her, I had a puppy called Indie for six months and then I took on a golden retriever called Ikea, initially with the plan of starting him off before handing him over to another puppy walker. However, Ikea had only been with us for a week when he got a severe attack of diarrhoea and vomiting. This is quite common with puppies so I fed him a bland diet and waited for it to pass, but five days later it came back again and we had to get the vet in.

Tests were done and it was discovered that he was suffering from a bug called campylobacter, a zoonotic disease that can be passed from dogs to humans and humans to dogs. It meant he was unable to absorb the nutritional value from his food and he became increasingly unwell. The bug was on a five- to seven-day cycle so we would think he was getting better then it would come back again. Right through his puppyhood we had to watch everything he ate like a hawk, and be very careful not to get infected ourselves or to let Endal get infected.

Ikea was nine months old before his immune system was strong enough for him to have his puppy vaccinations, and at ten months we began to notice that he was a bit lame. It seemed he hadn't absorbed enough nutrients to build a good bone structure. Everything he did tired him out, almost like a person with ME.

At around ten to eleven months, the specialist said to me in the nicest possible way, 'You have to consider whether he's compatible with life. If this dog was ten or eleven years old, fine; but he has the brain of a puppy and the body of an elderly dog and I'm not sure if it's right to keep him alive.'

I was devastated because I'd become very attached to my poor sickly dog. He was sensitive, kind and gentle, and I could never have lived with myself if I'd had him put down before he was even a year old.

I went to talk to Canine Partners about him, and they said that there was no way he could become an assistance dog – he just wasn't strong enough – but they said I could adopt him as a pet if I wanted to. They warned me that the vet bills could be high with a dog like this, but for me there was no question that I would take him. He had become very much 'my' dog, where Endal was Allen's, and the dynamic worked well at home with the two of them. We signed the paperwork and I took Ikea home as a pet, not a working dog.

I loved all the puppies that came through the house and, amazingly, they all got on well with Endal. He's quite a laid-back character, happy to let someone else be top dog – although he won't be walked all over. It didn't seem to make a difference if it was a bitch or not, because all our dogs are neutered very young. The majority of the Canine Partners assistance dogs are male, simply because breeders tend to keep their female puppies to breed. When I did train a bitch, such as Gracie, I found they were busier and more independent than the male puppies. They could multi-task, whereas the boys just repeated the same thing over and over until it became second nature. I wouldn't say one was necessarily better than the other, but it amused me that the sex differences seemed similar to those between men and women.

It was always very emotional for me when it was time to hand over a puppy but I tried to prepare myself because I knew that was the deal from the start. All the dogs love their puppy walkers the most, and although they go on to work with other people quite happily they'll be beside themselves with glee if they bump into their old puppy walker somewhere. It's like children: they go to school and work with their teachers and maybe they'll grow to love a particular teacher, but they always love their mum and dad the best. We try to keep the puppy walkers in contact, if possible, and they might pass on some puppy pictures to the new owner.

Gradually I was doing more and more volunteer work for Canine Partners, and I was over the moon one day when they approached me and asked if I would like a full-time, paid position with them. It was a Monday to Friday, nine-to-five job, with decent holidays and a whole week off between Christmas and New Year. It suited me right down to the ground. I'd been happy to work there for nothing, so to be offered a salary for doing what I loved made me feel very privileged.

As a member of staff, I got involved in some other areas of the business I hadn't tried before, such as learning how to choose from a litter of puppies the one that will make a good assistance dog.

We would go to see a litter when the puppies were about six weeks old because at that age they were starting to show their individual characters. We were looking for a puppy that was not so bold that it would dash off and do its own thing, but confident enough that it wouldn't panic at any slight noise or new experience. We didn't want it to be too independent because then it would be wandering off all the time, but it needed to be able to learn quickly and play nicely. Above all, we wanted dogs that liked people and sought out human company.

To test their responses, we would start by taking the puppies, one by one, to a place they hadn't been before, maybe out in the garden, or a room in the house they weren't normally allowed into. We'd give them a quick cuddle then put them down in a corner and run and hide somewhere they couldn't see us but from where we could watch them. Some puppies would stay where they had been put down, get very anxious and even start crying. Others would get straight up and hurtle off in all directions, unconcerned about the fact they had been left alone. The ones we were interested in were the ones who would sit for a while then get up and start looking around the immediate area trying to find the person who had brought them there.

After about a minute, we would go up to the puppy and clap loudly to see what the reaction was. Some would ignore us and carry on with whatever they were doing. Some would approach us warily with their ears and tail down, overcome with fear and trepidation. Others would be delighted to see a person again and would come up close to try and jump on our knees and say hello, panting and licking our hands in their excitement.

We would play a game with them using a toy on a string to see whether they decided to pat the toy with their feet or grab it in their mouth. It is thought that the dogs that go in with their mouths have a hunting instinct while those who use their paws have less of the chase drive, so they were preferable. Some were frightened of the toy and refused to play at all, perhaps growling at it, and those puppies were going to be too timid for us.

There was a fine line when it came to courage. If, say, you dropped something and it made a loud noise, some puppies would run and hide, while others wouldn't bat an eyelid, almost as if they hadn't heard it. The ones we wanted would be startled then turn round to check our reaction, and if we didn't seem alarmed they'd decide that it was fine and wouldn't panic. It was important to choose dogs that would be calm when exposed to the outside world, but responsive to external stimuli and alert to danger.

As I talked to doggy people over the years, though, I realized that for every theory there is an equally strong counter-theory. If there are three dog experts in a room and two of them agree on something, you can bet your bottom dollar that the third won't.

As I immersed myself in my wonderful new job, Allen became engrossed in dealing with all the media requests for stories on Endal. By suppertime we always had a lot of news to discuss with each other. We were starting to like each other again, I mused one day. I never saw that look of irritation and sheer hatred on his face any more. We were arguing much less and talking much more.

Of course, he still drove me crazy. He had learned to use computers, so once I was working full-time I asked him if he could do the weekly food shop online. 'No problem,' he said, and then I'd get home to find him playing a computer game, and there was no food in the house because he'd completely forgotten.

'Man with a head injury!' he'd say, tapping his forehead, when I berated him for this, but I was getting wise to the excuse. Of course it was true that there were huge blanks in his memory and parts of his past that he will never remember again, but I was also aware that he was now perfectly capable of remembering some things, and he used a notebook to remind himself of tasks he mustn't forget.

Sometimes he would over-react when I accused him of not doing something and I'd realize he was fibbing when he said he'd forgotten; he just hadn't wanted to do it. So when he 'forgot' to do some chore I'd asked him to, I felt justified in getting annoyed about it.

I was working full-time but I had to come home and do the housework and cook the dinner and then help the kids with their homework, and at weekends I had to be the one who cut the grass, climbed ladders to clear gutters of dead leaves, painted the woodwork and so forth. I got quite cross about it on occasion and had a moan to one of my girlfriends – and she pointed out that these were normal marital problems. He was behaving just like a lot of other men the length and breadth of the country!

I laughed out loud. It wasn't anything to do with his injury or his memory loss; it was a classic problem that was being aired in households around the world wherever there was a working wife and mother. It was touching to think that we had 'normal marital problems' again! That seemed like a huge achievement after coming through all the other abnormal problems we'd had.

Allen wasn't the man I had married any more and I was beginning to accept that he never would be again. We still fell out over all kinds of silly domestic issues, and when we fell out he could be very childish in the way he reacted, and very selfish. He'd sometimes talk too much in company or make rude comments to people, but he was learning to shut up when he caught a particular warning expression on my face.

I began to see the wheelchair as a real barrier to intimacy in our relationship. Even if I'd wanted to, I couldn't walk down the street holding his hand, and I would never again have a slow dance with him at the end of an evening out. We didn't have much physical contact at all, but the fact that we were having conversations was something I hadn't even dreamed of a few years earlier when he was first discharged from the Navy. We never talked about the past or the future; it was just about what we were doing that day, or what the dogs had done, or what the children had done – but it was enough. It felt like being in a team again.

Meanwhile, he was proving extremely successful in his new media career, posing with Endal at photo shoots, giving interviews and being filmed by TV crews from all over the world. It seemed as though every day some new opportunity came along, and as his life broadened out beyond the four walls of our home, so his mental capabilities seemed to expand to deal with the new challenges. And the happier and more fulfilled he became, the easier it was for the kids and me to live with him.

CHAPTER TWENTY-FOUR

Allen

After Endal got the Millennium Dog of the Year award, I started getting daily emails and phone calls asking for press interviews and wondering if camera crews could come and film us. I just said yes to everything because I couldn't see any harm in it. It was all good publicity for Canine Partners, and Endal obviously enjoyed performing for the media. His tail would wag with all the attention and he'd be watching eagerly to see what they wanted him to do next.

If any of them offered a fee, it went straight to the charity, but if they offered Marks & Spencer's liver and bacon treats – his favourite – they would get an extra-special performance out of him. He still kept an eye on me in case I needed anything, but he would also stick close to the director, alert for his next cue like a true professional.

Even when we were out working, I'd try to make it fun, maybe hiding behind a bush so he had to find me – and he would sometimes play tricks on me, grabbing my hat from the rucksack I keep on the back of the wheelchair and pretending to run away with it. I've never come across a dog with such a great sense of humour.

If we were stuck indoors for any length of time, Endal would be happy if he was allowed to watch animal documentaries on television; any programme with animals in it had him glued to the screen.

The interviewers had a whole range of questions for him. Some wanted to know if he'd ever had a girlfriend, and I replied that he was neutered very young so he never had a girlfriend as such, but that there was a German shepherd called Brontë he was very keen on. She was the boss of all the dogs at the training centre and Endal was scared of her, but he'd creep up to her on his belly and roll on his back in submission. She'd pretend to growl but Endal still loved her to pieces and trotted over to her whenever we saw her at the Canine Partners centre.

They asked about his favourite foods: cheese, doggy biscuits, turkey, and liver and bacon treats. They asked about his favourite smells: port and fox pooh. They asked about his pet hates: barbecues – he'd always hated the smell of smoke – and Sandra and me arguing, which makes him slink off sadly upstairs. Sometimes this new-found celebrity status got to seem ridiculous but I couldn't see any harm in it. If people wanted to read about him, why not let them?

In 2000 Endal was invited to go on the London Eye at an event to launch an internet site called 'Pet Planet'. He wasn't afraid as the big wheel took our glass pod up to 135 metres above the River Thames, but he was a bit bemused to see the birds he would normally have tried to chase flying along below us. I knew as I watched him gazing out of the window that all he was thinking was: OK, where's the food?

We were invited to Harrods as part of a promotion to give away copies of *Dogs Today* and to shake a collecting can for Canine Partners. Mohamed Al Fayed came over for a chat and put £100 in my can, which was incredibly decent of him. It was only three years since his son's death in the car crash with Princess Diana and I felt very sympathetic towards him. No matter what the media said, he was basically just a grieving father. After that, Endal and I were regularly invited back to do promotions at Harrods and every Christmas we would pose for a photo with Santa Claus in their Christmas grotto.

Lots of film crews wanted to witness the cashpoint skills that had brought Endal to the attention of the media, and he was endlessly obliging. He seemed to sense what they wanted, and would pause at strategic moments to let them get the perfect shot. I remember one crew got us to do several differ-ent takes and each time I was withdrawing a tenner from the cash machine but because it wasn't my bank I was getting charged £1.50 per withdrawal. And then disaster struck! They asked us to leave the cash in the dispenser while they filmed it sitting there, and all of a sudden the machine sucked it back in. I hadn't realized that if you don't take the money within a certain amount of time, it's reabsorbed. That was an expensive day out for me!

A Japanese film crew came to visit us at home. They had heard that Canine Partners dogs were taught to open washing machines and take the washing out so they asked if I could get Endal to demonstrate that. Now, this wasn't a skill that I had ever taught him so I was a bit concerned but I said we could have a go.

We put on Endal's jacket (after a rebranding exercise, all Canine Partners jackets were purple now) and I demonstrated opening the washing machine door and pulling out some clothes, then asked Endal to do it.

To my astonishment, he went straight up to the machine, opened the door, pulled out the washing into a basket positioned just below and pushed the door shut, before turning to me for a treat.

'I thought you said he couldn't do that!' the cameraman exclaimed.

'I didn't think he could …' I was as amazed as them.

'It was all a bit too fast, though,' they said. 'Do you think you could ask him to do it again so we can get it all on film?'

Endal was happy to oblige and pulled out the washing several times, opening and shutting the door with ease. When Sandra came home that evening and I told her what happened, she didn't believe me. Of course, when I asked Endal to do it again to show her, he uncharacteristically refused. He'd had quite enough for one day.

She saw him in action not long after, though. Our washing machine gave up the ghost just before Christmas and Sandra and I went to a big department store to buy a new one. When we arrived on the correct floor, a salesman came over and asked what he could do to help.

'I'm looking for a new washing machine,' I said. 'But it has to be one that my dog can open.'

'Pardon?' he stammered, his eyes popping out of his head. He obviously thought they'd let the lunatics out of the asylum.

Sandra chimed in. 'We're looking for a washing machine the dog can open. Is it all right if we try a few?'

'Sure,' he said, looking round desperately to see if any other colleagues could come to his rescue.

Endal went down one row and nudged open every single washing machine along the way. There was a toy department nearby and some children noticed what he was doing and came over to watch, clapping and squealing with excitement. Endal turned into the next row and I noticed that one of the machines there was half price because of a special Christmas offer. 'Please let him be able to open that one,' I prayed, and sure enough he could.

The poor salesman watched helplessly as Endal stuck his head inside the machine and pulled out all the hoses and connectors.

'We'll take it!' I said, and the man sighed with relief. I'm sure he just wanted to get us out of the shop.

Several film crews that came to visit us wanted to see Endal doing the shopping with me. At Canine Partners, dogs were trained to pick goods from the shelves when their owner flashed the beam from a miniature laser pen on to whatever they wanted. I had a pen like that and used it sometimes but Endal was familiar with most of the items I normally bought from our local grocery shop and could pick them out by name. Rolls, tomato soup, baked beans, brown sauce … he'd walk up to an item then look round at me for approval before picking it up.

The film crews soon found that Endal would get it right every time and it was more likely to be me who caused them to need a second take. With one crew, we had rehearsed a selection of items that Endal was to pick up, including some from high shelves he had to jump up and rest on his front paws to reach, and others from low shelves. One of the items was 'rolls' and we'd rehearsed it four times and knew exactly where they were. But once they were filming, for some reason I said 'bread' instead of 'rolls' and Endal only hesitated for a moment before walking further down the aisle and selecting my usual loaf of bread for me. Nothing got past him.

We had one film crew – American, I think – who wanted to spend twenty-four hours with us. They even filmed Endal asleep in his bed, wakening briefly to look up and check I was still there, then going back to sleep again. The next day they filmed us walking through the town and at one point I reached round to get something out of the rucksack on the back of my wheelchair. I didn't realize that I had dropped my canvas hat on to the pavement at the same time.

Endal picked it up, put it back in the bag and carried on walking without even coming round to ask for a reward. It was only when I looked back at the footage later that I realized what he had done. It's not often that animals will do something for you without at least looking for praise, and it's unheard of for a Labrador to miss the chance of an extra food treat!

It was all getting a little mad and one day Sandra came home after a hard day at work to find her house cluttered up with cameras and lights and so forth. A crew from an American news channel was still filming when the children got home from school. We sent them upstairs to play but, whatever they were doing, they were making a bit of noise.

'Can you get those kids to quieten down?' someone asked Sandra. 'They've just ruined the last take.'

And she snapped, 'Right! That's it – everyone out!'

She didn't care who they were. It was family time in the Parton household, and before they knew it they were out on their ears. The film crew scurried around dismantling their equipment and took to their heels. That producer came back the next day with a bunch of flowers and an apology.

Next, Endal was asked to appear on *Blue Peter*. What happened was that the Crufts winner in 2000 was American and they had to jump on a flight straight back to the States. However, it was normal practice for the Crufts Best in Show to appear on *Blue Peter* and they had left the slot free for him. Funnily enough, I'd been at the press office at Crufts that day chatting to someone and bemoaning the fact that Endal could never win an award at Crufts because he's been neutered and you have to be an entire dog to win.

Back home that evening, I got a call asking if there was any chance Endal and I could appear on *Blue Peter* the next day and help them to fill the doggy slot? I said, 'Yes, of course,' then came off the phone and asked Sandra, 'How on earth am I going to get to Television Centre in Shepherds Bush tomorrow morning?' She was busy working but we managed to find a local taxi who agreed to take me.

The presenters Konnie Huq and Simon Thomas had promised viewers that a very special dog would be appearing on the show. They started with some archive footage of Endal getting money out of a cashpoint machine and helping me to cross a road, and then we came out into the studio to chat to them. It's all filmed live so if the dogs start barking or chasing the studio's cat, it will appear on TV sets up and down the country. Endal behaved perfectly when the cameras were rolling. They gave him a couple of challenges, such as finding my gloves in my rucksack and bringing them to me, and he did them perfectly. Then he was awarded his *Blue Peter* badge, and I thought it was ironic because, according to Mum, when I was five years old I had written in but hadn't got one. Now my dog had one instead!

After filming was over, we were just sitting there when the *Blue Peter* cats ran across the studio and Endal immediately set off after them, wanting to play. There were two other dogs running around as well and some model volcanoes got a bit trashed but no one seemed to mind too much.

They're all doggy people there. Before we left, I let Endal have a tiddle in the *Blue Peter* garden, just for the sake of it.

As I've said, we agreed to just about every media request. Endal even went on the local radio station, where he was a natural and barked on cue for the presenter. It was lovely to have all the attention, but I had to be careful that he didn't overdo it. Once the film crews left, he had to carry on working until I went to bed. He might be exhausted, and I know *I* often was, but he would still fetch things for me, open doors, pick up anything I dropped and hang around taking care of me. If he lay down for a rest, some part of him would always be touching the wheelchair so that he would wake up if I moved.

To keep up with all the media appointments, I had to learn how to get myself around. There was no way I could learn to drive because my reaction times weren't good and I wasn't able to calculate the speed at which cars were travelling. It used to drive Sandra crazy that I'd clutch the dashboard when she was driving me somewhere.

'What is it?' she'd snap.

'Aren't you going too fast?'

'I'm doing twenty-nine miles an hour, Allen. It's fine.'

So driving was out of the question for me. I could manage the local buses without a problem because they had a disabled ramp to help me get on and off; I found a good local taxi company with nice roomy cars to accommodate the chair, Endal and me; and I also learned to get on and off trains. If there was a step up to the carriage, a guard would come and place a ramp for me. When they introduced push-button door opening on our train service, Endal was quick to learn how to operate the buttons, to the astonishment of other passengers. As soon as the light came on, he'd jump up and nudge it with his nose. There was a fast train from nearby Petersfield up to London Waterloo, which meant that I could easily get up to the city for interviews and media events, and I began to use it regularly.

Every new journey I managed added to my confidence. I could never have gone without Endal, but I knew he would protect me if anything happened – as he soon proved.

One dark evening after a day's filming at a studio in London, we were making our way back through the streets towards Waterloo station when a man came out of the shadows and walked towards me. As he passed I saw him checking out my rucksack. He got to the end of the street, then turned and came back in our direction again. I unhooked the bag from the back of the chair, clutched it to my chest and wheeled myself faster. The street we were in was deserted so, my heart pounding, I made towards a road several blocks further along where I could see traffic flowing.

Suddenly Endal turned towards the man and started barking louder than I'd ever heard him bark before. The man stopped and Endal advanced towards him without any let-up in the barking. I began to worry that the man might produce a knife or something but after a moment's hesitation he turned and legged it off into the night. Without Endal, I've got no doubt I would have been mugged and there's nothing I could have done to prevent it. You're very vulnerable in a wheelchair.

Soon there was to be a more famous occasion on which Endal would rescue me and this time there would be witnesses.

We always enjoyed our annual trips to Crufts, held at Birmingham's NEC, but in 2001 the competition was delayed due to the outbreak of foot and mouth that swept the countryside in the early months of that year. It was May before it was finally held and Sandra was too busy with work to come along. Undeterred, Endal and I went along with the Canine Partners team to help on their stand.

By this, our fourth Crufts, we had our little routines and places where we liked to chill out. There was a mattress where we could lie down for a rest near the press centre, and little patches of grass where I took Endal for a wee. 'Better go now!' I'd say, and he'd obligingly empty his bladder. We booked in to a dog-friendly motel not far from the NEC and met some colleagues for dinner on the first night, 24 May.

Afterwards we left the restaurant to cross the car park back to our chalet-style room. The light was fading and there were sounds of revelry from a nearby pub. All of a sudden I heard a car engine starting and before I knew it a car had reversed out of its parking spot and straight into us. In the split second when I realized what was happening, I tried to push Endal clear but then the car hit my chair and toppled me out on to the tarmac.

I think I lost consciousness briefly, winded by the fall. I only know what happened next because there is CCTV footage of it all.

Despite having taken quite a blow when the car hit him, Endal sprang into action. First of all, he grabbed my jacket in his teeth and pulled me on to my side, into the recovery position. Then he retrieved a blanket that had been on the wheelchair and pulled it over me. My phone had got knocked under the car as I fell, but Endal found it and placed it by my head. When I didn't start talking into it straight away, he realized more help was needed and he ran across to the pub, barking furiously to get attention.

I had come round by this stage but was dazed. I'm not sure what the driver of the car was doing, but I think he was very shocked. At any rate, it was Endal who got someone to summon an ambulance, and then he came back and waited by my side till help arrived. I tried to talk to him to show him I was all right but I think my voice was very shaky. I looked round and saw that my chair was badly buckled where the car's wheel had gone over it. I was lucky it hadn't gone over me as well.

An ambulance drew up and the men checked me out where I lay on the ground, then they lifted me on to a stretcher and into the back. Endal immediately climbed the ramp to follow.

'We're not supposed to have dogs in here,' one of the men said, but they realized there was no way he was leaving. He was still wearing his purple Canine Partners assistance-dog coat, so they relented and let him come along.

Once we got to A & E, a nurse tried to stop Endal coming through to the cubicle where I was placed for assessment but he just wasn't having it. He planted himself by my side, less than a foot away from my head, where he could see everything that went on, and he wouldn't budge.

It was one in the morning by this time and a child was sobbing loudly in the next-door cubicle.

Poor kid! I thought. I wonder what he's doing in here at this time of night?

Suddenly Endal poked his nose under the curtain that divided us and stuck his head into the other side. The crying stopped immediately.

'Oh, there's a doggy here,' the child's voice said in amazement. The sight of a big yellow Labrador seemed to calm him down and the crying didn't start up again.

A nurse popped her head in. 'Isn't he lovely?' she said, stroking Endal's head. 'Would he like some water?'

'Yes, please.'

When the doctor came, he checked me for concussion and broken bones, but the only injury I'd incurred was bad bruising down my right side. The wheelchair was a write-off, though. Fortunately I had a power chair with me that was charging back at the motel, so I wouldn't be stranded.

I was taken back to my room in the early hours of the morning, thinking that was that. I rang to tell Sandra that I was all right, and she was relieved to hear from me because someone had already phoned to tell her about the accident. The next day a vet checked Endal and said he was OK. It had been a shock but it was all over as far as I was concerned.

CHAPTER TWENTY-FIVE

Sandra

Word of Endal's heroism spread like wildfire because it happened at Crufts, which was full of dog-lovers. Everyone was talking about it there, journalists pricked up their ears and it quickly made national news. Soon Allen was getting more interview requests than ever before. They all wanted to ask how Endal had known about the recovery position. Was he trained to do that?

The answer was that he wasn't. Canine Partners dogs were trained to go and get help if their owner fell unconscious. They knew that if it happened in the bath, they were to pull the plug out first. They had to run to wherever the nearest adult was and bark repeatedly, tugging on their clothes, until someone came. Maybe Endal was trying to tug on Allen's clothes to waken him up in the car park that night, but I think he just instinctively realized that lying on his side was the safest position for him.

They've done demonstrations for camera crews since then, and any time Allen lies on his back Endal will grab his jacket and pull him over on to his side. This is the recovery position recommended by first-aid professionals for anyone who is unconscious, because your airways are unobstructed and there's no risk of your tongue falling down the back of your throat and choking you.

Endal was always diligent, even when it wasn't necessary. Since he had learned so much about computers, Allen had started helping Canine Partners to set up new networks to connect their machines. There were times when that involved lying on the floor and stretching underneath desks to push plugs into sockets. Endal used to get really distressed when he saw Allen in that position and would try to tug him out. The staff and I stood in fits of laughter one day watching as Allen was trying to reach a socket while Endal was trying to pull him away. When he couldn't shift him, Endal began licking his face, making the job virtually impossible!

As the story of Endal's life-saving skills appeared in doggy magazines, he began to be nominated for all kinds of awards. *Dogs Today* readers voted him 'Assistance Dog of the Year'; he won an internet vote to be 'Coolest Canine'; and then in 2002 Bonio dog biscuits ran an entry form on the side of the boxes where people could nominate a dog to win a new award they had created called the 'Golden Bonio'.

Allen and I were invited to the Bonio awards ceremony at the Roof Gardens restaurant in Kensington. They put us up at a posh hotel the night before, and then we had a very nice lunch in the restaurant. The dogs all had bowls with their names on them and a team of doggy-watchers looked after them while we were eating. A BBC film crew was filming the day, and we sat through the long speeches as presenter Sue Barker announced the winners of all the different categories of award.

We'd been told Endal was getting something but they announced all the winners of the categories in the programme and he hadn't been called up. TV viewers could probably see the disappointment on our faces as the camera panned towards us. Had we come all this way for nothing? Allen hadn't had a drink up till then so that he would be stone cold sober if he had to go up to get an award, but at that stage he decided to start sipping his wine.

Then Sue Barker announced that there was one last award, for lifetime achievement, and it was being given to Endal in recognition of everything he does to make Allen's life easier. We sent Endal up to collect the trophy himself – a big golden bone – then Allen wheeled himself up the ramp to the stage and said thank you. I was so proud of them both that day. It felt like being at the Oscars! Allen was grinning from ear to ear, looking very handsome, and I felt a warm glow as I watched from our table. It was a lovely moment.

After that a local radio station gave Endal a 'Local Hero' award at a big smart hotel in Southampton. I remember someone else who was being given an award that day was a diver who had gone down to try and rescue the men stuck in that Russian submarine, the *Kursk*. It was a great honour to be in such prestigious company and Endal barked his appreciation for the radio listeners.

He won a Dog of the Year award from a charity called Pro Dog that fought for the rights of dogs. He won a Golden Bone award from *Our Dogs* magazine. And then came the one that meant the most to us: the PDSA Gold Medal, which is the animal equivalent of the George Cross. It's the UK's highest honour for animal bravery and the medal bears the inscription 'For gallantry and devotion to duty'.

Since 1943, the PDSA (People's Dispensary for Sick Animals) have been giving an award called the Dickin Medal to animals who displayed conspicuous gallantry or devotion to duty while serving with the armed forces. Named after the PDSA's founder Maria Dickin, it has been won by pigeons that delivered messages during the Second World War, as well as dogs that helped to find survivors in the rubble of explosions during the Blitz and horses that didn't bolt but stayed on duty after bomb blasts. Endal was nominated for a Dickin Medal, but because his courage hadn't been demonstrated during war-time they decided to create a peacetime equivalent, which they called the PDSA Gold Medal.

Three dogs were given the Gold Medal in 2002, the year it was introduced. Two of them – Monty and Bulla – were police dogs who had been injured in the line of duty trying to protect their handlers while they apprehended dangerous criminals. Endal's award was for outstanding devotion to duty and all his remarkable skills, in particular for getting help for Allen when he was knocked from his wheelchair despite the fact that he had been hit by the car himself.

The awards ceremony was at a police headquarters and Princess Alexandra, the Queen's cousin, presented it. Zoe came along wearing her school uniform, because of her school's links with the royal family, and she was chosen to present the bouquet to Princess Alexandra. We were immensely proud of Endal that day and, predictably, the award sparked off a whole new onslaught of media requests for interviews and photo shoots.

Other Canine Partners dogs won awards, of course, but in 2002 none had achieved as much recognition as Endal and it was fantastic publicity for the charity. He was becoming quite a figurehead for them, a recognizable symbol of the good work they did, and we took dozens of calls at the office requesting his presence at all kinds of events. Endal took all the celebrity in his stride with his usual good nature. He loved meeting people and showing off and would happily have turned up to the opening of a paper bag so long as there was a doggy treat for him in there somewhere.

Sometimes I held Endal's head and looked into his big brown eyes to try and see what made him tick. The truth is he had no side. He was a bit of a show-off who enjoyed demonstrating what he could do, but above all he was a sensitive, compassionate dog who genuinely liked helping people in need. That's his character. That's what he was all about. People warmed to him. And he loved Allen to the core, utterly doted on him with every fibre of his being. All the

Canine Partners dogs were loyal to their owners but they liked a bit of time off sometimes, while Endal gave everything he had to the job. I think he knew how much he had done for Allen, but I shouldn't think he had any idea how much he had done to help me as well.

CHAPTER TWENTY-SIX

Allen

There I was: paraplegic, brain-damaged, dyslexic, forget-ful, unsuitable for service in the military and often very grumpy, but it seemed I was doing one thing right at least. I was so proud of Endal that I wanted to tell the whole world about him.

Media requests kept pouring in. One offer that I accepted immediately was to take part in the BBC programme entitled *Airport*, where they filmed air passengers and staff going about their business. They wanted to film Endal and me flying to Manchester to see how easy it was for a person in a wheelchair to get on planes. The crew came to the house in the morning and filmed us packing and we had a bit of fun because I left the suitcase open on the floor as I turned to do something else, and Endal put his box of Bonios on top.

When we got to the check-in desk and they asked, 'Did you pack this case yourself? Could anyone have put anything in it without your knowledge?' the TV crew were cracking up remembering those Bonios.

They filmed us being lifted up to the aircraft on a little hydraulic lift, and Endal was completely unfazed by it. Two seats had been reserved for us, and Endal lay on the floor at my feet. During the flight, while I was being interviewed, I accidentally knocked part of my sandwich off the tray and Endal gobbled it straight down, which made for another comedy moment in the film.

I was delighted to find we could travel easily on our own through airports, meaning we could make longer-distance trips without Sandra having to take time off work to accompany us. During the flight, if it was a long one, I'd bring out Endal's kong and play with him. Sometimes I asked the stewardesses if he could stretch his legs, and they always agreed. Passengers sitting in seats further back in the plane were astonished when a dog suddenly trotted past them at 32,000 feet.

'Did you see that?' I'd hear them say. 'Do you think dogs are allowed up here?' And the kids would all ask me if they could give him something to eat. He'd have a great time.

I chose British Airways flights whenever possible because I could wheel the chair along their covered walkways directly on to the plane instead of having to be raised in a hydraulic lift. One day when I was flying to Scotland, there was a party on board who were doing a course to overcome their fear of flying. They'd had their morning talk about the different noises a plane makes and how it works, and now they were bracing themselves for the actual flight.

The doors were closed and we were taxiing from the gate towards the runway when an elderly woman at the back started screaming, 'I can't do this, I want to get off!' The head stewardess had just pulled out her equipment to do the safety demo so she put it down on the seat beside me while she went back to calm the woman.

I decided to put the lifejacket over Endal's head and take a quick souvenir photo of him, just for a laugh. I was busy focusing the camera when the terrified woman came charging down the aisle. She saw Endal in the lifejacket and stopped dead.

'I don't know what you're worried about,' I said. 'We're not even flying over water, and look at him!'

She started laughing.

'Do you think you could help us?' I asked glibly. 'I'm supposed to feed him a treat every hundred metres or so during the ascent to help his ears adjust, but it's tricky because I don't have much movement in my right hand.'

This was a white lie, of course. The feeling has never returned to my right side but I can use it all the same. It worked because the woman sat down beside us and started feeding Endal so many treats that his tail was wagging like a metronome.

The plane took off and Endal kept her occupied and stopped her from panicking right throughout the flight.

'I'm doing this course to get over my fear of flying so I can visit my grandchildren in Australia,' she told me.

'So when are you going?' I asked, smiling.

'Soon,' she announced.

A couple of months later, I was delighted to receive a post-card from Bondi Beach.

Sometimes I didn't even tell Sandra when I was going off to film for the day. After she threw that American film crew out of the house, I had promised always to ask her permission before letting anyone film there, but once I could travel inde-pendently I could go out to do meetings and interviews with-out her help, and it felt great.

Endal and I would go up to London, meet the film crew at Waterloo, they'd follow us around as we went into banks or shops or pubs and did our stuff. It really did wonders for my confidence to feel useful again and, what's more, to be in demand.

I remember one time a film crew met us at Waterloo to film Endal opening and closing train doors, getting in and out of taxis and so forth. At lunchtime they offered to take me to a posh restaurant but I said, 'Actually that wouldn't be much fun for Endal. He needs to be a dog again just now.'

Instead of our posh lunch we went to Hyde Park to let him have a run-around and chase a few squirrels while we sat on a bench and ate some sandwiches. The director watched for a bit then he said, 'This is really nice. We should try to get some footage of Endal running around like this.'

They stood up to discuss where the shots should be and Endal came over thinking he was on duty again.

'It's a bit windy,' the sound man was saying. He turned to his assistant. 'Can you get the boom mic out of my bag?'

Before the assistant could move, Endal had gone to the bag, pushed his nose in and pulled out the large furry microphone. They were all speechless and I was surprised as well. Earlier I'd noticed that Endal was interested in the mic, probably because it was grey and furry like a small animal, so I suppose he just tuned in to the name. That's the kind of dog he was. His brain was always switched on.

When I was away from home overnight, I could stay in hotels quite confidently knowing that Endal would look after me and keep me out of harm's way. If I fell asleep without switching the lights off and closing the curtains, he would do it for me. He could manage pull switches and push ones, and he didn't wait to be asked; he thought of what needed to be done and just went ahead and did it. I wouldn't have had the courage to stay away from home on my own without him.

When Canine Partners wanted to expand to cover the Yorkshire area, Yorkshire Electricity agreed to sponsor them, provided that they got plenty of local support up there. Endal and I went up to help raise the charity's profile and we made an appearance on Yorkshire TV's afternoon show and in a local pantomime. I've got photos of him meeting Snow White and the Seven Dwarfs – though he barked at the dwarfs, which was somewhat embarrassing.

Back at the hotel, I let Endal out for a walk on the grass outside and he must have trodden on a piece of broken glass because when he came back in the pad of his paw was bleeding heavily. I scooped him up and wheeled him across to the bed, then looked around for a *Yellow Pages* to find a local vet. There was one on a shelf in the bedside cabinet. I stretched but couldn't reach it from my chair, and before I could stop him Endal had jumped down and picked it up for me. There was blood everywhere and for a horrible moment the thought occurred to me that he might die. The wound really looked awful. What if he lost too much blood? It was as though a vice were tightening round my heart.

I bandaged him up as well as I could, then found a local vet on duty who said to bring him straight in. A kind taxi driver came all the way up to the room and helped me to carry him downstairs – and Endal was a big, fully grown dog by that stage.

His foot was still bleeding when we got to the vet's and lifted him up on to the table. It was a deep cut but the vet managed to stop the bleeding, using some kind of spray.

'Would he like a biscuit?' the vet said when he'd finished and, on hearing the magic word, Endal jumped down off the table to look for the promised biscuit, thus opening up his wound yet again. You have to be careful when you use the 'b' word around him because it always gets a reaction.

Finally, we were able to go back to the hotel, Endal limping heavily, and I felt as though I had been through the wringer emotionally. I hadn't had any dinner and I was exhausted, but all of that faded into the background compared with the horrible anxiety I'd felt for Endal. He was the most unselfish creature in the universe. Even with a sore paw, he would jump off the bed to try and help me by getting the phone book.

I looked down at the handsome, clever Labrador who had given me so much and my stomach just turned over. It was an unfamiliar feeling that I couldn't place at first. My chest ached as I watched him lying there with his sore paw, sleepy but trying to keep his eyes open to see if I needed anything. Then I realized what the feeling was.

Sandra had told me about a night when she sat and kept watch over Liam, aged three, when he was in hospital with suspected meningitis. She'd described the intensity of her love for him that night and I realized that I was feeling the same kind of thing. That aching sensation in my chest was actually *love*. I don't know if it is the same way I'd experienced love before the accident but it was an immense, overpowering feeling.

It was gradual, of course, but once I started rediscovering these lost emotions, I began to look at my children and realize how smart and funny they can be. I'd missed so much of their lives when our relationship wasn't good because they just got on my nerves, and I can never get that time back. But I began to want to get to know them better and understand what made them tick. For example, it used to bug Zoe that I could never remember her teachers' names, so I made a concerted effort to write them down and ask her about her day at school and take an interest. I listened to her practising her clarinet and Liam playing his drums and asked questions about their tastes. I'll never remember their first words and first steps but I hope I'll always remember the sound of them laughing at a TV show or messing around together in the back garden.

And I started to look at Sandra as a person again rather than a carer. One day I remember I noticed how pretty her eyes were, and another day I sat admiring her kindness to beginners at the puppy classes. Then I started noticing what a nice laugh she has. I began to watch her when she didn't know I was looking, and thinking about how lucky I was to be married to her, and how extraordinary it was that she had stuck by me all those years since the accident. I'd thought this before, but in an intellectual way, and now I really began to feel it emotionally.

It was as though Endal had opened a little window in my brain that let me care about the people around me again. For eleven years I had been shut in my own selfish world where I only cared about other people in so far as they affected me. Now I realized I was interested in them for themselves and it mattered to me what happened to them. It might not sound much, but it was actually a huge leap forwards.

CHAPTER TWENTY-SEVEN

Sandra

The media attention Endal and Allen got after the car-park rescue could be intensely annoying, especially when my private space was invaded by film crews with muddy feet, but the changes in Allen made it all worthwhile. He became happy and outgoing once he had a purpose in life again. He was playful and jovial and a world away from the taciturn, bad-tempered man who used to sit in the corner stony-faced when he was on weekend leave from Headley Court.

After a nice meal one evening we were sitting on the sofa watching TV and I slipped my fingers towards where his hand lay on the seat. Immediately he took my hand and squeezed it, and tears came to my eyes.

We carried on watching the show without saying a word, but we kept our fingers intertwined. Zoe came into the room at one point and I saw her noticing with surprise. She'd never seen her mum and dad like that before.

It was a tiny, seemingly insignificant moment, but it meant everything to me. It meant he was responding to me as a wife again instead of just as his carer, and I felt a surge of love for him.

After that, we started to become more physically affectionate with each other – just a cuddle in bed, or a quick kiss in the kitchen – but it was wonderful. There wasn't the high passion of the early years of our relationship but, from what I hear, no couple keeps that for ever anyway. We were companions who enjoyed each other's company for the most part, and that was pretty good going after all we'd been through.

One day we were at a Canine Partners event. One of the girls had just got engaged so there was lots of chatter about weddings. Someone asked Allen about our wedding and he said, 'I don't remember getting married.' It was just an offhand comment, something he was no longer concerned about, but it bugged me.

'You may not remember the first wedding but you'll remember the second,' I told him quietly, without thinking it through. He looked puzzled, not understanding my meaning.

I didn't pursue it at the time, but over the next few days I started thinking about the fact that later that year, in November 2002, it would be my nineteenth wedding anniversary – but only mine. How could it be Allen's? He couldn't celebrate something he didn't remember. Without memory, the vows he made back in 1983 didn't seem to count any more. Besides, he was a different person now and so was I. In the early days after the accident I sometimes I felt like shaking him and saying, 'You *must* remember such and such. How can you not?' but I had long since accepted that he really didn't. The events that are gone from his memory will never come back. I can show him pictures but then he remembers the pictures rather than the event itself. His mother still finds this difficult and says things like, '*Surely* you remember young so-and-so. He was at primary school with you.' Allen gets irritated because he would love to remember, but he doesn't and that's all there is to it.

When I said to Allen, 'You'll remember the second wedding,' it was a throwaway comment on the spur of the moment, but over the next few days I gave it more thought. You read about lots of people who renew their vows or have their union blessed and I realized I wanted to do something like that. I wanted a big party, with plenty of time to organize it because it had all been such a rush in 1983. I thought it all through before I broached the subject with Allen again.

'How would you feel about us getting remarried?' I asked. 'So that we have a wedding day you can remember.'

He looked startled at first, and then he said, 'Was that what you were hinting about the other day? Are you serious?'

I nodded. 'Perhaps we could look into it and see what we can do.'

'Yes,' he said thoughtfully. 'I'd like that.'

Soon afterwards some friends asked us round for dinner and by chance there was a vicar there, so I picked his brains.

'You can't get remarried,' he said, 'because you've never been divorced. That means you can't make your vows to love and honour in sickness and health again, but you could certainly have a renewal of the vows or a blessing.'

I wasn't sure that I wanted to do it in a church, though, because I didn't like to picture the wheelchair having to make its way down the aisle past the pews. That chair seemed to get in the way of our intimacy and I didn't want it being prominent in any ceremony. If I was standing up while Allen sat beside me it would emphasize the inequality between us. And anyway, we're not very churchy people.

I decided I didn't want to have the ceremony in one place and the reception in another, which would involve everyone decanting in and out of cars. I started looking round for a suitable venue, and I came across the Old Thorns Hotel, a beautiful seventeenth-century country house in Liphook, Hampshire, where they said we could have the service, a dinner and evening reception and any guests who wanted to could stay overnight afterwards. I took Allen to see it and he liked it.

'How formal do you want this to be?' he asked. 'Do we have to get all dressed up?'

'If it's supposed to be like a first wedding, it should be pretty formal,' I said. 'So yes, I want a big frock and I want you togged up as well, and the kids should be involved. How about that?'

'Let's go for it,' he said.

We booked it for 9 November, as close as we could get to the original wedding date of 5 November. That gave me plenty of time to find the right outfit, so I started dragging Zoe and my friend Lyndsey around with me for trips to wedding fairs. I didn't want a classic meringue dress with a veil, but I didn't have the confidence in my post-childbirth figure to choose a tight cocktail number. It took a while but I finally found the perfect dress and it was worth the wait. It was a gorgeous full-length ivory taffeta dress with embroidery detail across the bodice and a little jacket that was short at the front but had long tails at the back. I also found a pretty gold tiara to sit in my hair and complete the look.

Allen got a new black suit and a smart gold waistcoat and cravat that complemented the beading detail on my dress. Liam was dressed as his dad's mirror image with a cream jacket and black waistcoat, and Zoe's outfit mirrored mine. My bouquet comprised lilies, orchids and palm leaves sprayed gold, and I also hired a fabulous vintage car to take me to the hotel on the day. I planned every little detail exactly the way I wanted it, even briefing the photographer on where I wanted photos taken. Allen was a typical man, leaving all the organization to me, but I was quite happy to do it. In these areas, I knew best!

At our first wedding we'd only had a finger buffet because it was being paid for by our parents and they weren't terribly well off. This time I wanted a fabulous sit-down dinner, and I also asked for lots of balloons and a firework display. Hang the expense! We were going to put it all on credit cards – or, as Allen called it, 'On the never-never.' I wanted it to be my dream wedding, to show the world that Allen and I loved each other. We were only going to do this once – although I remembered thinking that the last time as well!

I was wondering about hiring someone to film the day when Allen was contacted by a producer from the Esther Rantzen show *That's Esther* asking if they could film us and make a TV special about our story. It seemed like a great way to get a professional-quality movie of the day and I was happy to tell the world about our remarriage, so we agreed. We couldn't have stopped the press coming along once word was out as some doggy journalists were on the guest list anyway, so we agreed that the *Daily Mail* could cover the event.

There was still the question of what form the ceremony would take, but I got a phone call out of the blue from the vicar I'd spoken to at the dinner party.

'I've been thinking about what you told me,' he said. 'I couldn't get you two out of my mind because what you want is so right. I can't legally remarry you in a church but I'd be happy to come up with a form of wording that satisfies every-thing you want if we can do it somewhere else.'

I told him about the Old Thorns and he said that would be perfect, so we sat down and agreed the wording together, making it as close to the actual marriage ceremony as possible, complete with the vows 'in sickness and in health', which were now incredibly poignant for us given everything that we'd been through.

'I've made a few tweaks,' the vicar said, 'just so it's legal. But nobody will ever know where I've made the difference.'

The night before the wedding, Allen stayed at the hotel while some of my friends came to the house to help me get ready. In the morning I went to the hairdresser's and got my make-up done; then I headed off to the hotel in the vintage car with the traditional long ribbons attached.

When we got there, Liam leaped out of the car and went and found a seat in the room where the ceremony would be, with his music player plugged into his ear. I had to go and remind him that he was supposed to be escorting me and giving me away and he went: 'Am I?' as if we hadn't rehearsed it all fully a couple of days before.

I didn't want Allen stuck in his wheelchair for the ceremony, so he was transferred to a special decorative chair, and there was another placed alongside it for me to sit in at the same level. I had tears in my eyes as we looked at each other and said our vows all over again. I just couldn't believe we had made it there from such dark times. It was a miracle really.

Zoe played a piece on her clarinet during the ceremony, a Chinese school friend of hers played the piano and then my little eight-year-old nephew read a beautiful poem about marriage called 'The Walled Garden'. The idea behind it is that in every marriage there should be a private place where you go together and shut the gate and in there you are not a mother or father, carer, worker or homemaker, you are just two people who love each other, concentrating on each other's needs: 'The time we spend together is not wasted but invested.' It's a favourite of mine and it seemed particularly appropriate for us.

The day flashed past after that. Our photographer took lots of stunning pictures, keeping them as informal as possible and making sure he included all the family. I didn't want the traditional groupings of bride and groom, bride, groom and best man, bride and groom with parents and so forth, but I was keen that everyone was in there. We had our dinner and Allen gave a short speech thanking everyone for coming, then in the evening there was the fireworks display and then dancing. For the first dance, I sat on Allen's lap in his power chair and there was hardly a dry eye in the room as we twirled round the floor. I can't remember what the record was; I was too busy kissing my second-time husband.

It was a perfect day, and I think all our guests enjoyed themselves. It was my sister Jennifer's fiftieth birthday as well so that made it doubly special. Really I just wanted to share everything with the people who were significant to us, and that's exactly what we did.

We had said that we didn't want any presents because we had all the toasters and fruit bowls we needed, but a lot of people brought us personal gifts and there were dozens of bottles of champagne to take home. We'd have supplies to pop a cork on special occasions for some time to come.

I know I wouldn't have been marrying Allen again if it weren't for the way Endal had changed him. He dragged him back from the depths of misery into a place where he was happy and could start to communicate with the people around him again. Endal offered him constant companionship and support in a way that I couldn't manage full-time. If Allen woke up sullen and argumentative and turned round to snap at me about something, I found it difficult not to retaliate even though I knew it was because of his brain injury. Endal just accepted him as he was and was happy to serve him no matter what, and in the end that's what made the difference.

The man I'd married in 1983 was highly intelligent and ambitious, and even with a brain injury Allen would never have been happy sitting twiddling his thumbs all day. Through Endal he found a new purpose in life and his world opened out as he realized he could make a difference through all his charity work. He never turned down a single request that came in. No matter what, if he could do it then Allen would.

We couldn't go away on our honeymoon straight away because just after the wedding was the awards ceremony where Endal was getting his PDSA Gold Medal, but once that was over we flew out to Boston. I hadn't had a honeymoon back in 1983 – just a week on the naval base at Rosyth – but some friends invited us out for Thanksgiving and I thought that sounded like fun. To our surprise, when we got to the airport we were told we had been upgraded to first class for the journey there and back and we were escorted to the first-class lounge where lots of wonderful food and drink was on offer. It was a perfect start to the holiday.

We stayed in Boston for the classic turkey and pumpkin pie Thanksgiving dinner with our friends, and then we drove down to Cape Cod for a few days on that beautiful seaside peninsula. The weather was mild and we had a lovely time driving around looking at the pretty clapboard houses, eating clam chowder and peering out over the sand dunes to the Atlantic breakers.

So now I was married again, although not to the same man I had married first time around. There had been three Allens in my life: the high-flying, infinitely capable yet romantic man I had first married; the angry, taciturn, selfish one I had nursed for years; and now the contented partner with whom I had a shared interest in our dogs. When I looked into Allen's eyes I knew he loved me, although he was no longer demonstrative or spontaneously affectionate. It wasn't the marriage I had thought I was signing up for nineteen years earlier but it was good in a different way. Together we would make it work.

CHAPTER TWENTY-EIGHT

Allen

Sandra made all the arrangements for our second wedding and I was happy to let her. It was her big day and as far as I was concerned she could have it just the way she wanted it. I kept pinching myself because I felt so lucky that she was still prepared to stick by me after everything we'd been through. I knew I'd been awful to her in the eleven years since my accident. I'd been moody and unresponsive for most of that time, and I hadn't any right to expect her to stay with me; I'm just incredibly fortunate that she did because I'd fallen in love with her all over again. I couldn't imagine my future without her in it.

When planning the wedding, I liked the fact that she wanted my wheelchair to be as unobtrusive as possible. I did ask her if Endal could be there because it was thanks to him that we were still together, never mind making this new commitment, but she said the day was about us rather than the dogs and in the end I had to agree. If they'd been there we'd have been distracted by them, instead of being able to focus on each other.

On the morning of the 9th, I woke up as usual and wheeled myself to the hotel bathroom where I realized I had butterflies in my stomach. My hands were shaking so much I could hardly fasten the buttons of my shirt. For me, of course, it was my 'first' marriage since I couldn't remember the other one, and I had all the nerves that every other first-time groom faces.

What if Sandra had second thoughts and didn't turn up? I comforted myself that at least if that happened I would still be married anyway.

In the room where the service was to take place, I transferred myself across to the decorated chair where I was to sit and someone wheeled my wheelchair away. It was at that moment, I think, that the significance of it all hit me. This amazing woman was about to confirm in front of witnesses that she wanted to spend the rest of her life with me no matter what. And when I turned to see Sandra walking down the aisle with our son, I just knew that it was right and that I wanted to spend my life with her.

There was hardly a dry eye in the room as we said our 'in sickness and in health' vows. Few people can have tested them as thoroughly as we already had, and there was a conspicuous sound of sniffing and people scrabbling in their handbags or pockets for tissues.

At the end of the day, someone asked me how I felt, and I said simply, 'I feel complete.' It was as though a part of me that had been missing was reattached that day. I still couldn't believe my luck that such an extraordinary woman should love me, but against all the odds it seemed that she did.

I woke up the next morning and turned to look at her sleeping in bed beside me and was filled with a warm glow. This is what I wanted for the rest of my life.

There was a flurry of TV appearances, because everyone wanted to ask about our remarriage. We appeared on *That's Esther*, and were interviewed on *This Morning* by Fern Britton and Philip Schofield. Endal and I went on *The Oprah Winfrey Show* via a video link, and we were interviewed by the bubbly Lorraine Kelly on GMTV. We met loads of celebrities, including Rolf Harris, Gloria Hunniford, Richard and Judy, and William Roache from *Coronation Street*. They were all lovely, but I have to say that the one person Endal really took to was Paul O'Grady. Paul is one of the most charismatic, genuine personalities I've ever met, and a real doggy person.

We were invited back on *Blue Peter* again in 2003, and this time at the end of the show they announced that Endal was being awarded a gold *Blue Peter* badge. I didn't realize then but I found out later that these are only given very rarely, to those who have performed an act of extreme bravery or represented their country in a major way. The last person to get one before Endal's award was the Queen, who had received it while touring the BBC studios in 2001. It was a lovely gold-plated badge with the ship logo on it, and you get a letter along with it to say that it is genuinely yours and not something you bought on eBay (a real sign of the times).

Gradually Endal was becoming known outside the immediate doggy world. I was looking for a taxi in London one day when a woman came up to us and said, 'That's Endal, isn't it? How's Sandra? Isn't she with you today?' She'd read an article in a women's magazine about our second wedding and it was such a romantic story that it had stuck in her head.

She just chatted to us for a few minutes then continued on her way to work. I felt very strange, as though my life was in a goldfish bowl, but I was going to have to get used to it.

At the next Crufts, a group of Americans came up to us and said, 'Hey, is that Endal? We've just been watching a movie about him on the flight over.'

I think it had been a documentary called *Dogs with Jobs* that had been made for the National Geographic channel and they cleverly decided to show it on the flight that was landing in Birmingham on the day Crufts opened, obviously guessing there would be dog-lovers on board.

One of the buyers for the Harrods pet shop went out to an expo in Chicago and when she got to her hotel room and turned on the TV, she found there was a programme about Endal on air. She knew him already through the charity promotions we did at Harrods but told me it still felt bizarre to switch on American TV and see him!

Truth is, we did so much filming that I tended to forget what we had done. I'd be sitting watching television with

Sandra and a clip would come on with Endal, and she would say, 'For goodness' sake, when did you do that?'

'Can't remember,' I'd say, tapping my head. 'Man with a head injury!' The old excuse still worked.

I think she was just pleased we were busy and staying out of mischief. Sandra's always been a person with dozens of projects on the go at any one time, and so have I. Back before the accident we made our own decisions about our careers and hobbies and, although we were very close, we never tried to influence each other or stop each other doing anything. For example, Sandra didn't voice a single objection when I volunteered for the Gulf War.

It had been one of the strengths of our relationship that we had full, busy, independent lives, so that when we were together at home again we always had plenty to talk about. It felt to me as though we were getting back to that dynamic once more and as though the relationship was becoming more equal than it had been since the accident.

I can't bear being dependent on other people. I hate it if anyone tries to push my wheelchair or do anything for me that I'm capable of doing for myself. I don't think of myself as 'disabled' even though my legs don't work. Obviously there are certain things I can't do, and my memory still lets me down, but I reckon I don't do too badly on the whole.

CHAPTER TWENTY-NINE

Sandra

Liam and Zoe thought it was pretty cool that their dad was appearing on TV, and Zoe would want to join in whenever she could, although Liam hung back a bit more, as I did. Usually I was happy for Allen to deal with all the media demands but just occasionally I said, 'Hang on a minute, I want to be involved in that one.' I certainly wanted to be there if they were talking about Allen's and my relationship or our second wedding, but I didn't have much time for the rest. A few women's magazines requested interviews with me and I was happy to do that because they do your hair, put you in nice make-up and clothes and take some lovely photos!

I'm not as public a person as Allen. I don't mind giving a talk or a presentation on behalf of Canine Partners, but at a photo shoot I'm more likely to be the person standing beside the photographer waving a doggy toy to make the dog look at the camera.

I go to Crufts every year – the only one I've missed in the last ten years was the time that Allen got run over in the car park – but Allen and I do completely different things when we're there. He's got lots of networking to do with all his media and charity work, whereas I stay on the Canine Partners stand and just deal with any people who stop off with queries about our work. I hardly see Allen from beginning to end, but that means we've got plenty to chat about afterwards.

Endal was very much Allen's dog and I was happy about that, and about the fact that I knew he was 100 per cent reliable. No matter whether he was tired or limping, you could absolutely rely on him to do whatever you needed him to do. He was very brave and delighted to take on new challenges, such as TV appearances and flying in aeroplanes. My dog Ikea, the golden retriever, was more wary of the cameras, but he was top dog at home just because Endal was so easy-going and submissive. Ikea was more likely to defend his own space and less keen on sharing. They didn't fight with each other, though; we were lucky that way. And as I've said, the children absolutely loved the dogs. If they were at home for an evening, they'd be down on the floor rolling around playing with them. I do think it's good for children growing up around dogs, because they learn all kinds of caring skills.

Having recovered from the digestive problems in his puppyhood, Ikea was diagnosed with thyroid problems just a few years later that would mean him taking medication for the rest of his life, but he was always a very willing, sweet dog, despite his health issues. Ikea is more intelligent than Endal, in my opinion, although I'm sure Allen wouldn't agree. The two dogs used to play a game together where one of them grabbed a toy from the other and ran around the table to get away. When Endal was chasing he would just keep running round and round in circles, but if Ikea was chasing he would stop and turn round so that Endal cannoned into him, and Endal would look at him as if to say, 'Oh! How did you get there?'

Liam left school in 2003 and got a job at Waitrose, where he quickly started climbing the managerial ladder. He did lots of courses, included one where he learned all about fish, and was promoted to section manager before he had been there long. A couple of years later Zoe went to university where she did early-childhood studies and graduated with flying colours. She got a job as a nursery-school teacher and then took a course to become a hospital play therapist, dealing with children who spend time in hospital. They've both done very well, and I'm just relieved that they don't appear to be affected too much by the difficult time they had in their childhood after Allen's accident.

I took up some new hobbies once Allen and the kids became more independent and needed less of my time. One of these is scrapbooking, where you combine photos, memorabilia and stories in special scrapbooks. I started going on weekend courses and buying all the materials and accessories so that I can create a scrapbook for each of the periods of our lives. The conservatory is my work space and I lay out all my tools and materials on the table there and spend happy evenings and weekends working on my books. Partly I'm doing it for Allen, to try and give him an insight into all the things he can't remember, but I really enjoy the creative aspect of putting it all together into a beautiful book that we can browse through whenever we feel like it.

Since I became aware of how fragile memory can be following my husband's accident, it seems all the more important to preserve recollections for posterity. I suppose it's a way for me to come to terms with the huge life changes we've been through. I'm cataloguing and highlighting the good times while leaving out the bad – although the darkest moments will always be etched on my brain the way that acid etches a pattern on glass. I suppose you only appreciate how lucky you are when you have bad times to compare the good with – and we had many years' worth of both.

CHAPTER THIRTY

Allen

Managing Endal's career quickly became a full-time career for me as his awards and TV appearances led to requests for help from all sorts of charitable appeals. I set up an Endal website with lots of nice photos of him, and through the contact button there I started getting emails from people all over the world. It built up until there were between fifty and a hundred new emails a day and I tried to read them all even if I couldn't reply personally. Wherever we went, everyone seemed to know Endal already and they all came over to say hello.

One year at Crufts I got talking to two women who were handing out leaflets about an organization called Dog Theft Action. One of them, Margaret, had had her dog stolen and found the police didn't take it seriously. If someone stole your £250 video recorder, you'd at least get a police report and maybe they'd come round to do fingerprinting, but if someone steals your £2,000 dog the police don't do anything, she said, and that seemed wrong. I agreed to help them campaign for the police to give crime numbers and reports for each animal reported missing, and also supported their plan to get any agencies who deal with stray, injured or dead animals to carry scanners so they can at least scan the microchip in a dead cat or dog and contact the owners.

I was also invited to become an associate member of the Animal Welfare Group, an all-party government committee designed to promote the rights of animals, and a patron of Labrador Rescue, a charity that helps to find good homes for Labradors who have been badly treated or who just need a new home because of their owner's personal circumstances. Labrador Rescue have a great party every year that Endal and I try not to miss, because we are the judges for the Best Fancy Dress costume – a responsibility we take very seriously.

My early charity work was all for doggy charities but as the story got out about how I had been injured I began to get requests from military charities to give talks to men who had lost limbs or suffered spinal injuries that left them paraplegic or quadriplegic. I was happy to go along if they thought I could be of use, but I didn't realize at first just how powerfully it was going to affect me. Meeting guys who were going through the same experiences that I had gone through after my injury took me right back to those times.

Like me, at first they were all convinced they would walk again one day and resisted being labelled as 'disabled'. Like me, they became furiously angry when progress was slow and they often took their anger out on those closest to them. And, also like me, the majority of them became suicidal at some stage. It shone a harsh light back on some very dark years and made me realize just how impossible I must have been to live with – and I had had no idea at the time.

I sat and listened to their stories, letting them pat Endal as they talked, and when I looked into their eyes I saw a ghost of myself. Sometimes I felt a bit sick and panicky when I wheeled myself into a unit but I owed it to the men there to listen and keep calm and tell them a bit about my own story, if they were interested.

When you lose limbs, or lose the ability to walk, I think the process you go through is similar to bereavement. They say there are five stages in dealing with loss: denial, bargaining, anger, depression and finally acceptance. Many of the servicemen I spoke to were still in denial, telling anyone who'd listen that they'd be back on the front line within weeks. Others were in the bargaining stage, where they thought that if they did all their physio and worked hard at all the exercises they were shown, then things would turn out fine. I'd been there too. Anger and depression were commonplace, and some people got stuck there for years on end. I spent at least seven years on those stages myself and only really reached an acceptance of sorts after Endal came to live with me for good, towards the end of 1998.

I still feel angry that what happened to me was so unfair and random, but I can redirect my anger now. Sandra once asked me, 'When you arrive at a shop and you can't get into it, do you feel angry because you're in a wheelchair or angry about the fact they don't have disabled access?' In the past I'd been angry about being in the chair, but now I've switched to anger with the shop, which is much healthier.

I couldn't tell these men: 'Don't worry, everything will be fine.' I knew it wouldn't be. The trick is learning to put negative emotions behind you and get on top of the blow that life has dealt you. Spinal cords don't suddenly mend and limbs don't grow back again. Instead of regretting the past, you need to find a way to look for what is right in your life rather than what is wrong, just as I had done through my relationship with Endal. Lots of men don't manage it.

I was always happy to make public appearances for the British Legion, a charity that provides support for serving and ex-servicemen. They've done so much for us over the years. Through Housing 21, they put a roof over our heads when we were turned out of naval quarters. When my manual wheelchair broke and I was told there was an NHS waiting list of ten weeks to get a new one, the British Legion sent someone round to measure up the same afternoon and I received a brand-new chair from them within two weeks. They're an amazing organization and I do whatever I can to help them.

The King George's Fund for Sailors and the Royal Naval Benevolent Trust bought me my first power chair back in 1998 when I was getting Endal. People were worried that I wouldn't be able to exercise him without one but at that time they cost £7,000 and the Parton coffers would never have stretched that far.

I'm not crazy about power chairs, because what happens when you're stuck on top of a hill with the dogs and your charge runs out and you don't have a mobile phone with you? You can't ask some wee old dear with a Yorkshire terrier to push you home because power chairs weigh about 16 stone and I'm 12 stone myself, so it just wouldn't work. My chair has never died on me dramatically but it's stopped doing things like turning left when it runs out of charge, and the maintenance is expensive as well. However, it was useful to have a power chair for big events like Crufts, where I would have got too tired pushing myself all day. I had to take two chairs along so there was another one I could use while the first one was charging.

Endal and I often helped out on the Soldiers, Sailors, Airmen and Families Association (SSAFA) stand at Crufts, along with a guy called Danny, who had become a friend of mine. Danny was the army handler of a springer spaniel called Buster, who had won the Dickin Medal back in 2003. While on service in Southern Iraq, Buster had found a large stash of arms and explosives hidden behind a false wall in the home of an insurgent and had thereby saved the lives of countless numbers of soldiers in the region. His handler, Danny, was a cheerful, friendly guy with a good sense of humour and we hit it off from the start, while Endal and Buster were always happy to play at chasing each other round the SSAFA stand.

Buster and Endal were invited to take part in an exhibition at London's Imperial War Museum about Animals in War – the different roles they have played in different wars over the years. There was an engraving in the museum that really affected me; it said, 'War only ends for the dead,' and I thought about how true that was. For people like me, stuck in a wheelchair, the battle continues every single day. For the families of the disabled, it doesn't end when the guns go quiet, because they will have to cope with the repercussions for ever.

In 2004, Canine Partners were asked to take a team up to meet the Queen at Windsor Castle and tell her a bit about our work. I was overjoyed when they asked if Endal and I would come along, although sadly Sandra wasn't part of the delegation.

We drove up there in a minibus and were led out to the castle's stable yard, where they had laid ramps to make it wheelchair accessible for me. The Queen appeared and some of our young puppies did a display of their skills, then I was asked to come up in front of Her Majesty and tell her a bit about my experiences.

She seemed genuinely moved when I told her my story. I talked about the guilt that injured servicemen feel that they are no longer serving their country. You leave Portsmouth standing on the top deck of a ship, with banners waving and a festival atmosphere, then you skulk back in, wounded, through an obscure airport and are put in hospital and finally given a war pension, and you feel ashamed somehow, almost as if it were your own fault you got injured. The Queen was very understanding, and I found her to be a genuinely sympathetic human being. She took a real liking to Endal and kept petting him as we were talking.

It's Queen and country you serve when you're in the armed forces, so it was especially nice for me to meet her. What's more, I got a lovely letter afterwards saying that she had been very touched by our visit.

I was also very proud when the British Legion asked me to be the face of the 2007 Poppy Appeal. They took a photo of me in a wheelchair being pushed by Poppy Man, the giant figure made out of poppies, and it appeared on billboards up and down the country, with a caption pointing out that there are 900,000 injured servicemen and women in Britain today. It's a phenomenal number. I always go out shaking a collecting can in the run-up to Remembrance Day but it was good to be able to go one step further.

Endal and I first got involved in Remembrance Day back in 2003 when we were asked to lay a wreath at the war memorial in Portsmouth after six military policemen who had trained at the Chichester barracks were killed in a gun battle in Iraq. When I agreed to the request, Sandra went very quiet.

'Will you come along?' I asked.

'I'd rather not,' she said, turning away.

I had to question her for some time before she finally explained that Remembrance Day is a very poignant day of the year for her, because it never fails to remind her of what she has lost.

That was a wake-up call for me. I can't remember our relationship before my accident and I never will, so I only know what Sandra has told me. I'm aware that she used to depend on me emotionally in a way that she can't do now. I used to solve problems for her in a way that I can't do now. We used to be passionately in love in a way that we're not now. I don't feel this loss because I can't remember how it was, but I have to be sensitive to the fact that she does.

So on Remembrance Day she goes shopping or to visit her mum or sisters, while I go to whatever ceremony I'm linked to that year, and we meet at home later. As the engraving says, war never ends except for the dead.

CHAPTER THIRTY-ONE

Sandra

I had a full-time job, two growing children and a house to run so I didn't often get involved in Allen's media campaigns and charity appeals, but I was happy to accompany him on any overseas trips he was invited to make. In 2003, a delegation from the Japanese Hearing Dogs Association came over to visit Canine Partners to see how we selected and trained puppies. They were starting to do the same thing in Japan but they kept meeting with resistance from society because out there the extended family is supposed to look after a disabled person rather than a charity or the state. They decided to invite a bunch of disabled people who use assistance dogs from around the world to try and spread the word in Japan about how much difference the dogs can make, and Allen was one of the people they invited.

There were dozens of deaf and blind people there, particularly from the USA and Canada, and as one of the few able-bodied people I got roped into helping with all sorts of things, such as getting them to the meeting halls, finding things they had lost and running around getting drinks and food for everyone. I'd be rushing about getting orange juice for the blind people then having to tell them where it was: 'It's in front of you, at two o'clock.' Meanwhile, I was shouting instructions at the deaf people: 'We've to be in the conference hall at ten o'clock sharp.' In the end, I was pulling deaf people around and shouting at the blind ones and getting in a complete muddle.

Although it was a culture shock, it was lovely to make friends with so many people from other countries, and the following year, when we were invited to the International Association of Assistance Dog Partners in Phoenix, Arizona, we went along to catch up with our old pals from Japan. It was a very useful conference for me workwise, learning about training methods in the US and other countries, as well as being a social event. What's more, we managed to fit in a trip to the Grand Canyon, which was every bit as stunning as I'd expected.

The following year, the IAADP conference was in San Diego, and while we were there Allen became obsessed with touring round trying to identify sights that he'd visited when he was there with the Navy back in the 1970s. He'd spent a year there and was adamant that he should remember things, but he didn't. He wanted to go to the docks and check out all the ships, and he wanted to go to the zoo, and everywhere he went he got wound up that things had changed. He couldn't remember exactly where their ship had been docked, and he got lost because the road layout was different, and he became such a pain about it that we had a huge row.

'This is just stupid!' I raged. 'I'm not going to spend my holiday walking up and down streets like this.'

We were silent in the taxi back to the hotel. I understood that he wanted desperately to jog his memory but it wasn't going to happen and he had to accept that. Anyway, we made up before long and had a lovely afternoon there.

We didn't row as much as we had back in the nineties – probably no more than any other married couple – but he could still dig his heels in and be very stubborn and prickly. If he takes offence at someone, that's it – they're blacklisted and he will hold a grudge for ever. I go up like a rocket and calm down again just as quickly, but he will go up like a rocket and let it fester for days. He needs to go back over things again and again to try and prove that he was right in the first place, and sometimes when he gets very stressed his health can suffer. Because of this, I always try to stop myself getting angry and blowing up. But it was hot that day in San Diego and I'd just walked along one too many indistinguishable streets!

It's taken a long time for Allen to understand that the kids and I were damaged by his accident as well as him, but there are signs that he does. He works as a volunteer for an organization called Pets as Therapy (PAT), for whom he visits hospitals, hospices, residential homes and military schools with Endal, and he often makes a beeline for traumatized children in these environments. Children respond incredibly well to Endal and seem to come out of themselves when stroking or playing with him.

I hadn't asked much about this work, and then one day I read an interview Allen had given to *Your Dog* magazine, in which he was talking about his experiences with PAT and his own life history. He said, 'I volunteered to go to war and you take the consequences of that decision. But for a while, I think my children felt the Gulf War had returned a crippled stranger to them and not their dad. In a way I had died for them.'

I had tears in my eyes as I read it. He's never said that to me and it must have been very hard for him to accept. But when I read that article, I was delighted to see that he does understand a bit about what his family have put up with over the years. The kids really suffered back in the 1990s when they didn't have a dad any more and they couldn't have a normal social life either, while their mum was frequently preoccupied and exhausted. They just accepted it without question; that's how it was and there was nothing they could do, but I feel sad that they lost a lot of the carefree part of their childhoods when that four-by-four overturned back in 1991.

Allen's speech has now returned to normal – far from being stilted, you frequently can't shut him up. His short-term memory is much improved but his emotions are still subdued and his ability to empathize with others has never really come back. My job is quite stressful and I often come home from work feeling drained, but I don't get the emotional support I would like from him. Even if I've told Allen there are problems at work, he won't remember to ask me about them, or think of making me a cup of tea and telling me to put my feet up. The weight of everything rests on me. If I don't cut the grass, no one will. If the house needs to be painted, I can't rely on Allen to find a painter and get quotes and sort it out – I have to do it myself.

He has annual medical assessments related to the war pension but the verdict now is that they don't foresee any more changes and his current condition is for life. I don't think he's ever fully accepted that and I know I haven't.

Obviously I'm aware that he's not going to get up out of his chair suddenly and walk down the street but I think families always retain hope. I remember as a nurse that even when people are taking their last breath, the family are still going: 'Come on, hang in there, there's a party next week.' They can't let go, even when the dying person is ready. I suppose I feel that way. I have to believe his condition will improve one day and I won't give up that hope.

I read a depressing article about research into the long-term effects of head injury and it said that there is evidence that severe trauma to the head increases the likelihood of someone getting Alzheimer's disease. There is a direct link, because the head injury causes lesions on the brain. In a way, it is as if Allen already has a form of Alzheimer's, but I am terrified that this could get worse as he gets older, and I know he is scared of his condition deteriorating.

What would be wonderful is if it could go the other way and he could get back just a little bit more memory. I know that's the hope that he clings to as well, that one day the pockets of memory that come back to him might start to join up instead of being unconnected events without any context. I would love for that to happen but I can't see signs of it at the moment. His memory is very much about the here and now and by tomorrow a lot of what he does today will be gone. I live with him and I still can't begin to imagine what that must be like. But in a lot of ways it must be easier for him than it is for me.

CHAPTER THIRTY-TWO

Allen

Endal has always loved children of all ages, particularly ill or vulnerable ones. When we were invited to visit a home for autistic children, I knew they would enjoy meeting him. It can be difficult for people with autism to relate to human beings because they aren't able to read the social signals that most of us take for granted, but with Endal none of that matters. He doesn't put any stock in social rules.

When we first walked into the room, I got him to perform some of his wide range of barks, all at different commands from me, and that got their attention. It made them look outside the little protective shells they exist inside.

'Does he bite?' a little girl asked.

'Not once in his whole life,' I said truthfully.

Nervously they came forward to stroke him and he lowered his head to let them. We showed him playing games with his kong, and picking up things I dropped, and the kids were totally engrossed. Some of them wanted to hug him and I was worried they would squeeze too tightly but Endal put up with it all uncomplainingly.

When strangers come to our house, he will bark at them at first, as if letting them know that they are on his territory, and then, so long as I am relaxed with them, he calms down and ignores them. With the autistic children he didn't bark at all except when I gave the command. He was gentle and patient and we left them all happy and giggling.

The organization CHATA (Children in Hospital and Animal Therapy Association) asked me to bring Endal along to a holiday camp where terminally ill children are given a week of lovely experiences. We often used to turn up for their 'animal days' where the children get to pet all kinds of animals, and Endal enjoyed showing off the full range of his skills and being the entertainer. He's not horrified by physical deformity, so kids who have lost their hair to chemotherapy and are puffed up with steroids just look like kids to him. It doesn't enter his head that someone looks different. He walks up and finds a way to get their attention and they all end up falling in love with my big yellow Labrador.

An armed forces charity asked me to come along to an event they had organized for the families of men who had recently lost their lives in Iraq or Afghanistan. When we arrived I could see the hurt, anger and bewilderment on the children's little faces and wondered what on earth I could do. There was one girl in particular who, the helpers told me, hadn't spoken a single word since she'd been told about her father's death.

Endal has this unerring instinct for homing in on the most vulnerable person in a room, just as he homed in on me at the Canine Partners centre way back in 1997. He quickly noticed the silent little girl and obviously decided he wanted to get a reaction from her. She was ignoring everyone, turning away from us with abrupt, dramatic gestures, and Endal started copying her. She looked up; he looked up. She looked down; he looked down. She noticed what he was doing out of the corner of her eye but didn't want to react, so he kept going: putting his head to one side, shifting, even lifting his paw when she raised a hand to rub her face. Before long, she started moving deliberately to test him. He kept copying her and I saw a smile creep on to her face as she realized the power she had. Finally, the whole situation was so comical that she burst out laughing and the barriers came down.

Endal walked up to her and she got down on the floor and flung her arms round him. The helpers whispered to me that it was the first time they had seen her smile since her dad died. I decided to go over and have a word.

'He's copying everything you're doing,' I said, 'so I hope you're not going to do something rude like burping.'

She giggled, and we started to chat. I told her that Endal had a friend called Ikea back at home and she wanted to know more about how they got on. I described what they were like together, and then I said, 'Endal is missing his friend. Are you missing your daddy?' And she looked down and nodded. 'Give Endal a big cuddle,' I said, and she did. It was a very moving moment.

I don't know what made Endal decide to copy her body language – it's not something I had ever taught him. It was just an instinctive thing he tried to get through to a lost and sad little girl, and it worked. It was one more example of 'the Endal effect'.

Endal encourages people to feel warmth and affection again in the same way he did for me: by being totally non-threatening and non-judgemental and just offering a level of communication that it is impossible for them not to respond to. I'm always very proud and humbled when I see him reaching out like that. Other people might get the benefit of the Endal effect for a few hours or an afternoon, but I was lucky enough to get it for his whole life, more or less.

The core of Endal's life has been his devotion to me, which is absolute. He will put up with just about anything so long as I am nearby. He sits quietly for hours on end in radio and TV studios waiting till we go on air. He endures long train, car and plane journeys. He repeats his cashpoint and shopping skills over and over again for the benefit of photographers. In February 2008 Endal launched the first-day cover of the Royal Mail's working dog stamps and had to be photographed holding a letter in his mouth. We travelled up to Hyde Park where they had set up a fibreglass post box and Endal had to walk up to it and post the letter about fifty times before they were finally satisfied that they had the shot they wanted, but he didn't complain or refuse to do it once. That's just how he is.

If I have to go to the toilet without him and ask someone else to hold his lead, he will sit gazing in the direction I went until I get back, and no earthquake or hurricane could shift him from his post. When I have to be lifted up to an aeroplane on the hydraulic lift, a stewardess will usually walk Endal up the steps for me and he sits on the top step peering out until I'm beside him again. Even when he has a nap, he'll make sure some part of him is touching my chair so he can waken if I move. If I ever have to go out somewhere without him, he's not happy about it but he will manage so long as it's not for more than two or three hours.

I'd like to think I have earned this devotion, but I haven't. No one could. Endal would lay down his life for me in a heartbeat, as he's shown on the occasions he has protected me in the past without any thought for his own safety. In the early years, I was surly and ungrateful and took him for granted. Once I had learned to love him, I tried my best to be a playmate and to make sure he has everything he wants. I don't think dogs should be our slaves and I hope I've never treated him that way. I would never have let him do so much media work if it wasn't completely obvious that he loved showing off and really enjoyed all the challenges. I know he's had fun doing it.

After Endal's tenth birthday in December 2006, Sandra tentatively asked me if I had thought about what I would do when it was time to retire him. He still occasionally went a bit lame, he was going slightly deaf and he definitely got more tired than he used to. Ten is quite elderly for a Lab, so she was right that we had to think about it, but I resisted at first. On the one hand I realized that I was going to need a new dog in order to retain all the independence I had achieved, but I just couldn't face thinking about life without Endal.

There was no way we could bring an adult dog into the house because it would upset Endal and Ikea. Even an eighteen-month-old who had been through the Canine Partners training would put their noses out of joint. We were going to have to bite the bullet and take on an eight-week-old and start from scratch; but I knew that if we got a puppy I was going to be tied to the house for a while and would have to give up all my trips round the country while I was training it, and that was hard to accept.

We talked and talked about it and meanwhile Sandra mentioned to the people at work that we were looking and asked the breeders they worked with to let us know if there was a suitable litter.

I was quite clear that I wanted another yellow Labrador and that I wanted a boy. It wasn't that I was looking for a clone of Endal. They've cloned some dogs in the States for owners who wanted an exact replica of their much-loved pets, but as far as I'm concerned it would still be a different dog even if it was genetically identical. It would grow up with different life experiences and develop a different personality. No dog could ever mean as much to me as Endal because he came into my life at its darkest depths and pulled me up to the land of the living again.

'We'll call the new one EJ,' I said. 'Short for Endal Junior.' We also agreed that there should be a good overlap period so that EJ could learn from Endal what I needed and how to go about things. I wasn't optimistic that we would find a dog with a tenth of Endal's qualities, but I accepted that it was only fair to let him retire, so we started looking around for suitable candidates.

I began to worry that I might forget Endal one day after he's gone, because my memory is still terrible, so I commissioned a portrait of him by the artist Nigel Hemmings. He specializes in paintings of dogs, and in showing the relationship between dogs and people. I was very clear that I wanted the picture to show the view that I have of Endal's face looking up at me beside the wheelchair with that adoring expression he has. Nigel came round to the house and spent a day taking hundreds of photos and we looked at them all together. In the end he decided on one main image surrounded by a montage of others: Endal with his front paws on my lap; using a cash machine; getting a tin off a shelf; and opening a train door, amongst others. I couldn't have been more pleased with the final painting; it truly captures the dog I know and love.

Sandra has suggested that I make a scrapbook of Endal photos and memorabilia, but I find it hard to get round to this. I suppose I can't accept yet that he won't always be there. It will be horrible if I ever forget him, but after my accident I had forgotten my wife and children, and I still forget the name of our next-door neighbour and what I did just a few hours earlier. I forget to pay bills and buy milk. The other day I scribbled a phone number I needed on the back of an envelope then shortly afterwards I posted it in a postbox. It's like a slide rule: if I do something at one end, I'll be forgetting something else at the other. My brain will always be unreliable, so I suppose I should prepare that scrapbook, just to be sure.

CHAPTER THIRTY-THREE

Sandra

It was summer 2008 when we got a call to say there was a litter we might like to come and inspect. Allen and I drove over there together and had a look. As soon as we arrived one puppy came straight out of the litter pen with mud all over his head, so we nicknamed him 'Dirty Head'. Instinctively I thought to myself that he was the one; he seemed to have more character than the others.

Allen was very quiet, just sitting and observing, so I did the usual Canine Partners tests on all three boys in the litter. We took them out into a field and two of them made a mad dash for freedom, but Dirty Head came over and tried to climb on to us, wanting to play. He was obviously the one that wanted to be with people and I said to Allen I thought we should take him.

'I don't know,' he said. 'We can't afford it. I'm not sure if this is what I want.'

'We've got to tell the breeder whether to keep him for us. It's only fair.'

'Can I think about it?' he asked.

I took the woman aside and asked her to keep him, promising that I would talk Allen round. It was he who would have to be stuck at home looking after a new puppy so I could understand that was something he had to think about. It was difficult for him to contemplate not being with Endal all the time, and besides he finds it very difficult to make decisions since the accident. He doesn't like change. I'm still living with magnolia walls because he's not sure whether it would work if we tried some different colours. If I ask him whether I can switch round the position of two kitchen units, from his reaction you'd think I'd asked if I could blow up the house. So he needed time to get used to the idea.

We went home and we talked about it but I couldn't persuade him to make a decision. The weeks went by and the breeder was getting quite cross but Allen was having real difficulty with the concept of 'replacing' Endal and no matter how much I tried to persuade him he wasn't budging. We reached the eight-week limit when the puppies were ready to go to their new homes, and I spent the weekend basically bulldozing Allen into it. I couldn't present him with a *fait accompli* because he was the one who was going to have to train this puppy and it's quite a consuming job in the early days.

Finally, after I told him he had run out of time and the puppy would probably go to someone else now, he made the phone call and said, 'Can we come and pick him up? This afternoon?' And that was that. A brand-new bundle of uncontained energy exploded into our peaceful household.

What was strange was that Endal seemed to know what was going on. People say you shouldn't attribute human emotions to dogs but I swear that Endal looked at this puppy coming into the house and thought: Hey, I can relax now. The next morning when Allen got up, Endal had a lie-in for the first time in his life. He had such a long sleep that we had to go and check up on him to see he was all right. It was the first day of his retirement and he'd decided to take it easy – and he had every right.

Of course, EJ couldn't work for Allen straight away. He had to learn the basics, such as toileting, sitting in his crate, not jumping up and barking, and that takes weeks to achieve. Allen has always used different voices to get each dog's attention, and he developed a high-pitched squeaky one for EJ that had me in stitches. He also started using a hand-held clicker. When there are three dogs in the house you need to be quite clear which one you are talking to and be able to make them stop in their tracks at any time, and Allen's got that down to a T.

EJ is a lively but bright toddler who seems keen to learn and will copy whatever he sees Endal and Ikea doing. If they pick up the post from the mat, next day EJ will rush to get it first. He'll probably slobber all over it and destroy it before it reaches us but the instinct to help is there. He watched Endal opening cupboard doors for Allen in the kitchen when he was putting the washing-up away and one morning EJ just came in when I was there, pulled on the tuggie and opened the door for me. I looked round and Endal was watching from his bed, as if pleased with his star pupil.

I'd bought EJ outright from the breeders, and Ikea had been mine since he was a year old, but on paper Endal still belonged to Canine Partners. As he approached retirement we asked if he could be officially signed over to us, and they were happy to agree.

I know it meant a lot to Allen that Endal was finally 'his' dog and no one could take him away again. He was very moved. After that we talked about setting a retirement date for Endal when he would stop making public appearances and stay at home to rest more. We decided on a date just a few weeks later because he'd seemed very old and slow recently. But as it turned out, events were about to force us to take action sooner than we'd thought.

CHAPTER THIRTY-FOUR

Allen

In early September 2008, Endal and I had a busy week. Endal was presented with his wings by British Airways after having made fifty flights with them, so we squashed into a car and drove to Southampton airfield to get the award. Then we went up to London for a business-award ceremony in the Albert Hall, at which Prince Charles was present. Afterwards there was a school to visit, and at all these events Endal had to put on a bit of a show. The next morning when he woke up he could hardly drag himself out of his bed. He'd always had osteochondritis, of course, but he hadn't gone lame this badly for years, even after long photo shoots like the one for the Royal Mail. It wasn't just the front paws; he seemed to be having trouble with all four.

Endal had two vets – one for everyday things, and another who specialized in joint problems such as osteochondritis. We took him to see the joint specialist, who didn't know Endal as well as the first. There was a veterinary student with him that day.

'Let's see him walking,' the vet asked first, so we took him outside to the road and Endal managed to walk.

'Now let's see him trotting,' he said, but Endal froze completely when he tried.

The vet and his student had to lift him back inside and put him up on a table. The vet started feeling his legs, which made Endal yap with pain. He pointed out to us that both his left and his right front legs were very swollen.

'What's happened is that although the right leg is the main problem, he has tried to compensate by over-using the left and now it's in trouble as well. Because of this he's been trying to use the back legs and they're giving up too, making him quadrilaterally lame.'

As well as the leg problems, Endal had ongoing problems with ankylosing spondylitis, a disorder in which the vertebrae of his back were fusing together. A bone specialist from another part of the practice came in to join the discussion.

Sandra and I were expecting that they would perhaps increase his medication and ask me to let him rest for a week or two, so the next words came as a complete bolt from the blue.

'Basically,' the first vet said, 'if you were to ask me to put this dog down now, I would support that request.'

I couldn't believe my ears. I looked at Sandra. Her eyes were welling up and she was gripping the edge of her chair. I started to shake. I looked at Endal, worried that he might understand what we were saying, but he lay there oblivious.

'Quality of life is an issue here,' the vet continued, 'and while the threshold has not quite been reached, it could be very close.'

Neither of us said a word, but I suppose the vet saw from our reaction that this wasn't an option we were ready to consider. To me, it sounded barbaric. How could I think of killing my best friend and faithful companion when he still loved his life?

The vet continued, 'It's either that or a question of managing the pain as long as he has a decent quality of life. I can give you some morphine-based painkillers that will take the pain away but they'll make him quite dopey. I'd suggest you give them to him in the evening, before bedtime.'

Endal had been taking Metacam, a non-steroidal anti-inflammatory drug for easing arthritis in dogs, for years, and they said we should increase his dosage. The vet suggested he should sleep downstairs rather than trying to climb the stairs, that he should only have very short walks and, in particular, he should stop jumping up and putting his feet on my lap as I sat in the wheelchair – the classic Endal and Allen pose – because it jarred his joints every time he jumped down again.

'If we can manage the pain and make the lifestyle changes, he could have a bit longer – how long, nobody knows. You need to find the level at which the painkillers work but don't knock him out too much. There's a plateau the dog can find for himself.'

I concentrated hard, determined to remember every last instruction. Sandra seemed numb with shock still. I reached over and squeezed her hand.

Afterwards, we lifted Endal into the car and drove away in complete silence. Sandra was especially careful to avoid bumps in the road that might jar his joints. Neither of us could bear even to repeat the words the vet had said. We carried Endal into the house and laid him on his bed and gave him an extra-special dinner that night and lots of doggy treats.

The next day, Endal and I had been due at the Cold Wet Nose Show, a fun day out organized by *Dogs Today* where they have lots of prizes for things like the Waggiest Tail, Lovable Rogue and Prettiest Bitch. I had planned that I was going to announce his retirement in our acceptance speech but now I had to phone the organizers and tell them that we couldn't make it. The words caught in my throat as I said it, but they were very understanding.

News of Endal's problems spread and I started getting concerned phone calls from all sorts of people: a friend at Labrador Rescue; a journalist I got on well with at *Dogs Today*. Judith Turner, Endal's puppy mummy, heard the news and came over to visit, and Endal was overjoyed to see her, getting up from his bed to come over and lick her in his delight.

We started him on the painkillers but not on massive doses. We wanted to take the edge off the pain but not medicate him to the extent that he would stop feeling any twinges and might do something stupid like trying to chase a squirrel or swim across a lake. You can't cure arthritis but you can manage it if you're careful, and I think Endal realizes he has to be circumspect now. When we go out to the park he plods along, stopping to sniff when he detects an interesting scent, but he won't chase cats or birds any more. He wants to but I think he knows in himself it wouldn't be a great idea.

When I take Endal and EJ out for a walk together, Endal lets EJ take his traditional place at my right side and he stands further out, protecting both of us. EJ absolutely adores him. When I open his crate in the morning, he'll go straight over to Endal and lick his face to say hello. I'd always hoped they'd have longer to work together, so we could go out and about as a threesome and EJ could learn from Endal how things are done – but it wasn't to be. Endal's just not up to coming out on trips with me any more. Ikea does more for me now than Endal does and EJ is learning fast.

It became a lot harder for me when Endal stepped down; I realized just how much he had been helping me with things that I wasn't even aware of. I felt very disabled without him. It was a complete pain when I dropped something and couldn't reach it, or needed to dig something out of my rucksack or reach up to pay for a pint in our local without his help. It was much slower to get on a bus, wheel myself to the front to pay the driver, then turn round and go back to park myself in the wheelchair space, and it meant the bus had to stop for longer while I did all this. I'm not confident enough to catch a plane somewhere and stay overnight in a hotel on my own without him, so I miss the busy social aspects of the life we were leading before. I'm getting more tired now though, and often fall asleep on the sofa in the evenings, with Endal beside me. He's earned his rest. All the signs are that EJ will be able to take over his role bit by bit and in a year's time I'll be able to get out and about again as much as I ever did.

EPILOGUE

Sandra

Every evening when I leave work at Canine Partners, I call Allen from the car on my hands-free phone. It's our catch-up time when we share the details of our day – where we've been, whom we saw. Allen tells me what he's got planned for dinner and maybe I'll make a suggestion about what vegetables could go with it. We talk about everything so that when I arrive at the house I can switch off. It's become part of our routine, and it's one of the ways I unwind from the stress of my job.

When I get in Allen will have the dinner on and EJ will be running around playing. He's learning fast but, like any toddler, he can still be incredibly foolish. I once saw him trying to steal a food treat out of Ikea's mouth but he got his comeuppance fairly quickly with a sharp bark and a nip. Endal is much more laid-back and even lets EJ climb on his back and wrestle with him. He's like an overindulgent parent, smiling as he watches his favourite child learning the ways of the world.

As our children grew up, Allen and I had thought we were long past the days of clearing up a massive sea of discarded toys in the evening, but we're right back there again now. EJ likes to take the fridge magnets and walk round with them in his mouth and I'll find them later hidden in his bed. I noticed a teddy bear's leg in the corner and had to hunt round the house to uncover the rest of the poor, disembowelled creature. And we both have to remember that it is no longer safe to rest a cup of coffee or a sandwich on the floor even momentarily. Everything has to be kept on high shelves as if we are protecting it from incoming flood waters!

Liam still lives with us, although you'd hardly know it from the amount of time he spends at home. Zoe has her own flat, but she will call on me if she needs a room repainted or a loan to get her to the end of the month, and she'll usually turn up for dinner a couple of times a week. They don't need us much any more and that means Allen and I have more time to be a couple.

Recently we decided to have a holiday on our own and, feeling like a bit of childish fun, we picked Disney World in Orlando. It was lovely to go on the rides and, like all these American resorts, they had excellent disabled access. One evening we went to a show at Sea World and before it started the compère asked, 'Are there any American armed forces here? Please stand up.' A few dozen men stood up. 'Any of their families?' The wives and children who had been with them stood up and I looked at them with interest.

'Any allied forces from Britain here?' he asked next, and of course Allen couldn't stand but he waved his hand. 'Any of their families?' I stood up all on my own and the people round about us turned to stare.

Finally, everyone in the auditorium rose to their feet and saluted us and afterwards they all wanted to shake my hand. It was a poignant moment for me. I felt very close to Allen, and pleased by the recognition that his naval career and the aftermath was something we had been through together. I was a casualty of war as well as him; I just didn't have a wheelchair as a physical symbol of it.

We don't often talk about the bad old years and I've blanked a lot of it out. If I do look back I'm always surprised how long we survived the worst. From August 1991 through to February 1998 when Endal came to stay was more often than not a living hell, and after that the improvements were only gradual. It all seems such a long time ago from today when we can jump on a plane and go on lovely holidays together as man and wife.

Even though Endal is retired, we still get invited to media events, such as the première of the James Bond movie *Quantum of Solace*, where we met Princes William and Harry. But most evenings you'll find us at home, just relaxing together. We've got two sofas but we indulge Endal by letting him lie on one of them if there aren't any guests. He dozes on his back, legs akimbo, looking very comfy and occasionally making gentle little snoring noises. His condition is stable now and he's enjoying a comfortable retirement. Allen transfers himself from the wheelchair on to the sofa beside me and, more often than not, we'll nod off after dinner. We agree we'll try to stay awake to watch a particular TV programme but it doesn't often work out that way.

In November 2008 it was the twenty-fifth anniversary of our first wedding and that made me stop and reflect on the huge life changes we've been through. The man I married in 1983 was an ambitious, competitive, high-flying naval lieutenant, with a wicked sense of humour and a deeply compassionate side. Today he is still competitive and he still has a great sense of humour but his life is focused on helping others through his charity work, and I'm so proud of everything he's achieved. In fact, I'm more proud of him now than I was when he was designing weapons systems in the Navy.

Allen will never remember our first wedding or anything about our history before 1991. He still forgets what he did yesterday, and uses the 'man with a head injury' excuse when I berate him for not picking up another jar of coffee from the shops. My 'second husband' is calmer than the man I married first time round – and I get to see a lot more of him than I did of the first! They're quite different people, but when I look at any friends' marriages that are still intact, their husbands have changed drastically over twenty-five years as well. We all have.

We didn't celebrate our silver wedding anniversary on the day, but in 2009 we are planning a cruise that will take us from San Diego down through the Panama Canal. Allen has described to me the way the jungle encroaches on either side of the ship, and it sounds beautiful.

I prefer to look to the future now instead of the past. We've been through a lot, but we've survived and now we have so many good things to look forward to. I'm lucky enough to have found the man I want to grow old with, and that is a great blessing. The fact that he's good at doing silly voices and training dogs to use cashpoint machines is just the icing on the cake.

Acknowledgements

With huge thanks to Liam and Zoe for their endless love and support, which enabled us to get through those very early and difficult days against all the odds.

Sandra would like to thank her mum, for bringing her up with the independence and perseverance that helped her to keep going when times got tough. With love to her sister Valerie, who died in 1991, and love and thanks for their help and support to sisters Jennifer and Marion.

Grateful thanks to the Royal School and Churchers College, which gave Liam and Zoe such a fabulous secondary education and provided lots of extra help when needed. And to the Royal Naval and Royal Marines Children's Trust, which funded Zoe's education.

Thanks also to a special group of organizations that were there in the family's greatest hour of need: The Royal Naval

Benevolent Trust, SSAFA (Soldiers, Sailors, Airmen and Families Association), Seafarers UK and the Royal British Legion.

Enormous thanks to everyone who helped to make the second wedding such a big success: Lyndsey and Trevor Edwards, who did a lot of hard work in the planning and organization of the day; Father John, the vicar who took the service; and to the staff at the Old Thorns who went above and beyond the call of duty to make it all go perfectly.

Finally, thanks to all the people who have helped to make the Allen and Endal partnership so special:

Endal's puppy parents Judith and John Turner, for bringing up such a remarkable companion who really has turned out to be one of the nicest guys in the doggie kingdom.

Barry and Sue Edwards, who were Endal's breeders.

The special team of people at Canine Partners for Independence who in those early days had the belief, trust and vision to put Endal and Allen together: Rosemary Smith, then Chairman of CPI, and staff members Heather Caird, Tessa Rush, Nina Bonderenko and Alison Whittock (now Keeling).

The 29th of May charitable trust which sponsored Endal's training.

Direct Line Insurance, which provided Endal's insurance.

Beverley Cuddy and all her staff at *Dogs Today* magazine.

The editorial team at *Our Dogs* newspaper.

Derek Wright for producing such a fantastic photographic record of Endal at work and play.

The PDSA for recognizing Endal's courage and devotion to duty through the award of the PDSA Gold medal.

The Kennel Club for its friendship, support and belief for over a decade.

Labrador Rescue South East and Central, for giving us the honour of being patrons of such an amazing charity staffed by such dedicated volunteers.

Dog Theft Action for allowing Allen to be Vice Chairman and giving him an opportunity to make a positive difference.

But most of all to the dog-loving public who have supported Allen and Endal throughout ... thank you all so much.